War and State Building in the Middle East

Governance and International Relations in the Middle East

UNIVERSITY PRESS OF FLORIDA

Florida A&M University, Tallahassee
Florida Atlantic University, Boca Raton
Florida Gulf Coast University, Ft. Myers
Florida International University, Miami
Florida State University, Tallahassee
New College of Florida, Sarasota
University of Central Florida, Orlando
University of Florida, Gainesville
University of North Florida, Jacksonville
University of South Florida, Tampa
University of West Florida, Pensacola

War and State Building in
THE MIDDLE EAST

ROLF SCHWARZ

University Press of Florida
Gainesville · Tallahassee · Tampa · Boca Raton
Pensacola · Orlando · Miami · Jacksonville · Ft. Myers · Sarasota

First cloth printing, 2012
First paperback printing, 2013

Library of Congress Cataloging-in-Publication Data
Schwarz, Rolf.
War and state building in the Middle East / Rolf Schwarz.
p. cm. — (Governance and international relations in the Middle East)
Includes bibliographical references and index.
ISBN 978-0-8130-3792-9 (cloth: alk. paper)
ISBN 978-0-8130-4474-3 (pbk.)
    1. Middle East—Politics and government—20th century. 2. Politics and war—
Middle East—History—20th century. 3. Middle East—Politics and government—
Philosophy. 4. Politics and war—Middle East. 5. Nation-building—Middle East.
6. Nation-building—Middle East—Case studies. 7. Middle East—Politics and
government—20th century—Case studies. 8. Politics and war—Middle East—
History—20th century—Case studies. I. Title.
JQ1758.A58S35 2011
320.956—dc23   2011028200

The University Press of Florida is the scholarly publishing agency for the State
University System of Florida, comprising Florida A&M University, Florida
Atlantic University, Florida Gulf Coast University, Florida International
University, Florida State University, New College of Florida, University of Central
Florida, University of Florida, University of North Florida, University of South
Florida, and University of West Florida.

University Press of Florida
15 Northwest 15th Street
Gainesville, FL 32611-2079
http://www.upf.com

For Marie

Contents

Illustrations

Preface

I have enjoyed thinking about the state, researching state building, and writing this book, in ways I did not anticipate. I encountered the idea of the state first while doing my Middle Eastern studies. I was told then that "in the beginning was the state" and all other things—politics, society, and economics—followed thereon. So I set out myself studying the state, hoping to disprove my teachers and colleagues, only to find the truth of Ibn Khaldun's observation that state rulers maintain their hold over government and their own dynasty with the help of clients and followers who grow up in the shadow and power of group feeling and whose relationships to the state rulers determine their welfare, security, and representation.

This book was written over a period of seven years. I spent most of this time in Geneva at the Graduate Institute of International Studies. Part of the time I spent researching in the Middle East and at Princeton University. During the last years, which I spent in Brussels and Rome working as political adviser on the Middle East and the Gulf region at NATO Headquarters and now at the NATO Defense College, I have been able to look at the issue of state, security, and welfare from the practical perspective. All this has helped me in trying to come to grips with the state, to refine my thoughts about the idea of a rentier state and its implications for state building more generally. I would like to thank the Ernst and Lucie Schmiedheiny Foundation and the Fonds National Suisse for their generous support in facilitating my travels to the Middle East and my stay at Princeton University during the academic year 2005–6.

Acknowledgments

In writing this book I have benefited from numerous discussions and comments from colleagues, friends, and family. I am greatly indebted to all of them for helping me sharpen my argumentation and weed out factual mistakes: George Abi-Saab, Sadik al-Azm, Mona al-Ghobashy, Marko Bandler, André Bank, Nancy Bermeo, Alberto Bin, Miguel Centeno, Khalifa Chater, Nancy Coffin, Michael Cook, Eric Davis, Cédric Dupont, Robert Finn, Denise Garcia, Gregory Gause, Sandy Guptill, Peter Haggenmacher, Grant Hammond, Sükrü Hanioglu, Sven Holtsmark, Jalal Hussein, Amaney Jamal, Oliver Jütersonke, Sun-Chul Kim, Jacques Paul Klein, Bernard Lewis, Ellen Lust-Okar, Urs Luterbacher, Stephanie Mazzola, Malik Mufti, Nasser Bin Nasser, Hardy Ostry, Roger Owen, Pierre Razoux, Michael Reynolds, Hamid Rezai, Thomas Richter, Oliver Schlumberger, Chris Schnaubelt, Philipp Stucki, and David Sylvan.

I would like to thank in particular L. Carl Brown at Princeton University for his help in arranging my stay there and for his time and extensive comments in the writing of this book. His comparative approach and his historical knowledge of the Middle East remain an admiration and a force of inspiration to me. A special thanks also goes to my friends and former professors, Riccardo Bocco at the Graduate Institute of International and Development Studies in Geneva, for his help with practical aspects of my stay in Jordan and for his in-depth knowledge of the Arab world; and Keith Krause, who followed this project from the beginning and who gave me valuable comments on every step of it. I would like to express my thanks and admiration to the late Charles Tilly for his patience and openness to discuss modifications of his theory of state building. I write this book also in his memory and hope that it will serve useful to students of state building.

And lastly I would like to thank my wife, Marie. Without her support and love this book could not have been written.

Introduction

The European state-building experience is the only case of sustained political development comparable in scale and scope to the one unleashed by the recent wave of state formation.

Thomas Ertman, *Birth of the Leviathan*

State making is more than sovereign authority over territory and it is broader than regime type. State making is complex and best captured in terms of the three core functions of any modern state: security, welfare, and representation. State making requires legitimacy of rulers and of political rule.

The famous dictum that "war makes states" has received renewed interest in recent years with the experience of state collapse and state failure in many parts of the world. Historical studies have shown that war and state making were closely linked in early modern Europe (Tilly 1975; McNeill 1983; Ertman 1997). Getting ready for war and waging war required power holders to get involved in actions that were also conducive to state making. This included the effective extraction of resources for waging wars. Extraction presupposed state control, which in turn required an efficient bureaucracy. In cases where there was little or nothing to extract from society, war making also required the promotion of capital accumulation. Through all this, the activity of war making required the growing strength of a centralized bureaucracy and the emergence of states.

The formation of states in the Arab Middle East[1] challenges standard assumptions about state making based on the "war-makes-states" theory. The Middle East has seen many violent conflicts, and war is perhaps even a defining feature of the region. Indeed, few regions of the world have been so profoundly shaped by war as the Middle East, and no fewer than 43 wars have been fought since 1945 (Jung 1997). Virtually every state in the Middle East has been exposed to war making of some kind. This includes classic inter-state wars, such as the wars between Israel and its Arab neighbors, the Israeli-Palestinian conflict, and the invasion of Kuwait by Iraq in 1990, as well as internal war making and civil wars, so prominent in the cases of Lebanon and Yemen, and instances of asymmetric warfare and local insurgency, as witnessed in Algeria, Morocco, Egypt, Saudi Arabia, and Oman at different moments in their history. And yet the four Arab states that have most been involved in wars—Iraq, Jordan, Egypt, and Syria—have not all followed the European path of state making: Iraq failed in its state-building experience, Syria developed entrenched authoritarianism, and Jordan and Egypt became weak states. In the Middle East, war has interacted with processes of state making in ways that differ fundamentally from the European experience (Heydemann 2000a: 9). Extraction for war making has not led to legitimate political rule, as wars were funded by foreign sources or rents of one form or another, with wars being fought with imported weapons, and peace settlements were negotiated and guaranteed by external powers (Ibid.: 23). And yet, war making has had profound influences on social process and transformation as well as on state making. A comparison of three Middle Eastern states that focuses on the impact of war making on state making indicates that rentierism[2] undercuts the "war-makes-state" mechanism that is supposed to induce state making. Rentierism serves as an obstacle to the formation of strong states that legitimately represent their citizens and leads to institutionally weak states which lack political accountability. But rentierism also gives life-support to weak states, as it allows state institutions and channels of patronage to continue providing general welfare; it thereby contributes to overall stability. This claim is as such not new and has indeed been affirmed by analysts of oil politics in the Middle East. What this book points out is that where military capacity has been paid for by rulers' rents and where war making has been employed as a strategy of state building, this had effects diametrically opposed to those of the ruler-subject struggles that characterized early modern Europe. In the Middle East, unlike in Europe, wars did not make states—they destroyed them.

State making can be defined as those processes that lead to the centralization of political power over a well-defined continuous territory, with a monopoly of the means of coercion (Weber 1922). State making is thus closely linked to the processes of bureaucratization, revenue accumulation, and centralization of the state. But state making also requires legitimacy of rulers and of political rule. Bureaucratization is a central feature of state making as it is the means by which the state monitors and regulates society, as well as the means by which it extracts revenues from society. Charles Tilly has captured this in his famous dictum that "war made states and states made wars" (1985: 170). The institutional mechanism that links the waging of wars and the expansion of states in Europe was threefold: political, administrative, and fiscal. Politically, it became necessary for absolutist monarchs to extend rights of representation in government to those capable of paying the taxes necessary to finance wars they wished to fight or felt compelled to be able to fight. The development of nationalism and the extension of political rights to wider society thereby became associated with states whose relative legitimacy permitted them to raise more taxes, build larger military capabilities, and fight more wars to victorious conclusions and thereby prevent their destruction as states due to the territorial expansion of other states. Burgundy, Flanders, Savoy, Geneva, and Venice are all examples of states that once flourished but then disappeared as independent entities in this competitive European system. The much larger and technologically sophisticated armies and navies of countries such as France, Germany, and the United Kingdom were able to conquer and defeat these smaller states. However, modern armed forces required more developed and effective administrative structures to extract resources (in terms of manpower, conscripts, and taxes) as well as to direct growth toward indigenous industrial and agricultural bases that could assure financial support. The use of these enhanced capabilities to prosecute successful wars then led to even greater administrative and political capacities to tax and extract other resources.

The connection between war making and state making is absent from most states in the Middle East. States have often been fighting the "wrong kind of wars" to promote state making (Sørensen 2001). The state-creating wars in Europe were largely territorial—designed either to protect existing states against invasion by their neighbors, or to extend state control over previously autonomous areas. In Europe, the territory was up for grabs. This is not the case for modern Middle Eastern states. Although many borders are artificial, the states' territory is given and assured by external powers.[3] In the Middle East it is the regime, and not territory, which is up for grabs. Autonomous processes of state making were largely denied by the European great powers (Lustick 1997). And yet, Middle Eastern states survived. In a competitive European-style state system, many such states—for example, Jordan, the United Arab Emirates, or the smaller Gulf states—would have probably been grabbed by powerful neighbors and incorporated into their territory. But states do not have to be great powers to survive, as these examples demonstrate. They can compete in the economic realm and also (albeit to a lesser degree) in terms of military might and war making.

Hence, Middle Eastern states stand in contrast to the authentically sovereign states that emerged in early modern Europe. Abundant oil revenues in the Middle East allowed a degree of militarization which would have been impossible to maintain if regimes had had to rely on domestic resource extraction for financing. Therefore this factor, far from stabilizing the process of state making internally, contributed to domestic state weakness (see also Barnett 1992; Chaudhry 1997; Crystal 1990; Gause 2002; Gongora 1997; Heydemann 2000b; Krause 1996; Vandewalle 1998). The domestic process of establishing an efficient bureaucracy from an efficient military apparatus—characteristic of early modern Europe—could not materialize in the Middle East. In some Arab states of today, large bureaucracies exist; however, these serve as a way of distributing rents and, contrary to the situation in Europe, not as an effective tool for extracting resources from society.

Rentier states are states that do not generate revenues themselves. They obtain and actively seek large amounts of international rents. Their political functioning depends on these international rents, which are usually understood to be income accrued from the export of natural resources, especially oil and gas, but also bilateral or multilateral foreign-aid payments, such as foreign development assistance. Strategic rents form the majority of state revenues in many small states in the developing world (M. Moore 2004) and indeed in some Middle Eastern states (Richards and Waterbury 1996). In these countries the majority of state revenues accrue from abroad, and the state generally does not depend on the populace for taxation revenues. Rentier states rely on allocation and redistribution of rents and hence display a political dynamic very different from that of states in which the government is sustained via extraction of resources and the taxation of domestic economic activity. Distribution, rather than extraction, becomes the primary function of governments. Rulers of oil states can thus avoid bargaining over citizen consent by seizing control of energy production, selling energy products on international markets, paying off their main local supporters with the surplus, and buying coercive means to repress any remaining grudging dissenters. Oil-generated wealth thus allows rulers to bypass consent and resistance. As oil wealth declines, governments have to adjust to maintain this bargain. They can either produce resources themselves or extract resources from their subject population, thus producing the long-term conditions for democratization (Tilly 2007a). In either case there is a close link between the fiscal and social foundation of political rule (Beblawi 1990: 87–88; Levi 1988).

In the Middle East, the concept of the rentier state was first applied to Iran (Mahdavy 1970). The oil revenues received by Iran enabled its governments to embark on large public-expenditure programs without resorting to taxation and without running into drastic balance-of-payments or inflation problems. The infrastructural power of the state was never put to the test by its society and remained considerably lower than in other states. Iran was a rentier state *par excellence*: it was neither economically productive nor endowed with steady economic growth and was characterized by a state apparatus de-linked from its domestic constituencies and from society. This created alienation within Iranian society which ultimately contributed to the revolution of 1979 and the failure of the state (see Ahmad 1982; Skocpol 1982). In the Middle East, the rentier effect is not confined to oil states such as Iran. Non-oil states obtain strategic rents via migrant workers' remittances, transit fees, and aid payments. Rents thereby cut across the whole of the Arab world and propagate a new pattern of behavior: rentierism (Beblawi 1990: 98). Many states have made rents conducive to state making by incorporating social groups into the regime: rents have allowed state institutions and channels of patronage to continue providing general welfare and have thus contributed to stability. Thus, rentierism has produced the twin phenomena of weak states and life-support for weak and fragile states. Failed states are therefore rare in the Middle East, despite expectations to the contrary.

According to a traditional understanding focusing on Max Weber's definition of the state as the holder of the monopoly on the legitimate use of violence within a given territory, rentier states can only be conceptualized and measured in terms of distance from the ideal Weberian type and thus usually fall considerably short of this definition. This is exemplified in the usage of terms such as "state weakness," "corruption" and "failed states." Therefore the strengths and weaknesses of rentier states can best be determined by taking a functional understanding of statehood. From Thomas Hobbes to Max Weber, the state is commonly seen as the provider of public goods and services.[4] Its basic functions are the provision of internal and external security, of representation and legitimacy, and of welfare and wealth. The core challenge for rentier states is to provide all three functions—security, welfare, and representation—at the same time. This book sets out to highlight the areas where Arab states are strong and where they are weak.

In recent years, scholars in the field of Middle Eastern studies have stressed the idea of state autonomy and the distinction between strong and weak states (Ayubi 1995; Migdal 1988; Owen 2000; Salamé 1987). Arab states, it was argued, possessed large bureaucratic apparatuses, but their regimes held weak legitimacy with their societies. Arab states are authoritarian, coercive, and aggressive but not necessarily strong and legitimate (Ayubi 1995). But how can one explain the persistence of current Arab regimes, given the weakness and fragility of the state? In this context, the notion of a rentier state has received particular prominence, and several scholars have shown how rentierism may lead to domestic coalitions conducive to stability of otherwise weak states (Brownlee 2002; Brumberg 2002; Herb 1999; Hertog 2008; Karl

1997; Schlumberger 2007; Smith 2004, 2007). In that sense, rentierism becomes a means of life-support for weak and fragile states.

This book is not a chronological history of state making in the Middle East, but rather an analytical account of the dynamics and trajectories of the consolidation of states in the Arab world since the late nineteenth and early twentieth centuries. I explore the various facets of state making and the interplay between external rents, war, and the adjustment of social contracts, and I advance an argument that links the way in which rulers acquire their means to rule with the quality of that rule. I analyze three states in detail: Iraq, Jordan, and the United Arab Emirates. Two of these, Iraq and Jordan, have experienced war making, while the other, the United Arab Emirates, has not. Following the Tillyan approach, we would expect the emergence of an institutionally strong state in those states that experienced war making. However, the contrary is the case, as war making led to state failure in Iraq and to the emergence of a weak state in Jordan. In the case of states without the experience of war making, the Tillyan approach would predict the emergence of weak states, but again the contrary is the case: in the United Arab Emirates, in actuality, we see the development of a legitimate and sustainable rentier state with embedded authority structures.

Three components frame the argument of the book and set the context for the country case studies pursued in the individual chapters. The first component relates to oil revenues: the abundance of these gives rulers the means to exchange consent for material welfare. Such revenues serve as an obstacle to the formation of democratic states, as stability rests on a social contract whereby welfare and security are exchanged for political representation. This is the case with the United Arab Emirates. Second, while rents inhibit the emergence of democratic structures, they also serve as life-support for regimes and thus hinder the disappearance of weak and fragile states if used for the incorporation of social groups into the regime and not for war making. This is the case with Jordan. Finally, where rentier states employ war making as a strategy for state making, this will lead to state failure and the breakdown of the rentier state. This is the case with Iraq.

Why these three states? What can the specific experiences of Iraq,

Jordan, and the United Arab Emirates tell us about state making in the Middle East more generally? I argue that they paint a rather gloomy picture for the entire region. All three states stand in contrast to the states that emerged in early modern Europe. Legitimacy is lacking, and the state remains a hollow shell. While these states are authoritarian and coercive in character, they display elements of institutional weakness because they are limited in their capacity to actively cope with the challenges posed by globalization and necessary economic reform. Their infrastructural power is limited to providing domestic security and, in times of abundant rents, general welfare. They lack genuine representation and consent. But state making requires legitimacy of rulers and of political rule. Rentierism has played an important role in structuring this character of Middle Eastern states. It helps to explain such diverse cases as tribal states in the Gulf (capital without coercion creates embedded authority, as evidenced in the United Arab Emirates) as well as the emergence of weak states in Iraq and Jordan. Indeed, I will argue—perhaps counterintuitively—that these last two are the norm when it comes to statehood in the Middle East, while the United Arab Emirates and the other small Gulf states are exceptions. This is in line with recent scholarship that has argued that, *contra* Max Weber, the "natural" state (North, Wallis, and Weingast 2009) does not monopolize legitimate violence but instead brokers an elite consensus in which armed groups tolerate domestic peace in exchange for rights to extract rents (Snyder 2010). This peace is sustainable as long as enough rents are available. Where states lack adequate resources for welfare, they will implode, succumbing to state failure. This is the case with Iraq but also applies to a few other states in the region, such as Algeria, Yemen, Somalia, Iran, and now also Libya (Lowi 2004; Skocpol 1982).

The selection of cases for this book was undertaken in accordance with a comparative research design intended to account for the levels of war making and of rentierism. In classifying the 17 states of the region, I chose cases in order to test two theories—Tilly's "war-makes-states" and standard rentier-state theory—against each other and to see how individual states in the Middle East perform against theoretical expectations (see table I.1, with case studies highlighted in italics). I have concentrated on selecting states that have not received prominent

Table I.1. Typology of Middle Eastern states

	Rentier states	Semi-rentier states
War making[a]	Iraq, Algeria, Libya, Oman, Palestine, Saudi Arabia, Syria, Yemen	Jordan, Egypt, Lebanon, Morocco
No experience of war	United Arab Emirates, Bahrain, Kuwait, Qatar	Tunisia

Note: a. A high level of military preparedness is counted as a high level of war making. Hence Libya is included in the war-making category since this country, in addition to having a high degree of military preparedness, also fought a short war with Egypt in July 1977. Saudi Arabia is also included as a state that has experienced war making due to the domestic coercive measures employed to pacify certain regions of the kingdom—which led one regional specialist to conclude that the "patterns of Saudi state building match the broadest sequencing patterns of state making in early modern Europe" (Chaudhry 1997: 98)—and due to its high degree of war preparedness. Oman follows Saudi Arabia and has also been involved in war making—during the Dhofar Rebellion of 1964–75. Finally, Yemen and Lebanon are included as war making states because of the internal conflicts that have characterized these states.

attention in the literature; hence, I avoided looking in detail at Saudi Arabia and Yemen (Chaudhry 1997), Qatar and Kuwait (Crystal 1990), Kuwait (P. Moore 2004), Algeria (Bennoune 1988), Libya (Vandewalle 1998), Syria (Perthes 1995), and Egypt and Israel (Barnett 1992), which have all been analyzed thoroughly in terms of state making. Instead, I have focused on states that have experienced war making extensively— Iraq and Jordan—as well as on an oil state in the Gulf region, the United Arab Emirates, that has not experienced war making, to contrast this.

None of the three states analyzed in this book relies on domestic resource generation. Like other oil-producing states around the world—Venezuela, Bolivia, Chad, Kazakhstan, Russia, Turkmenistan, and Uzbekistan come to mind—they avoid consent by relying on sales of monopolized energy supplies. Yet energy production does not automatically forbid consent: the oil-producing states of Mexico and Nigeria, for all their democratic deficits, do actually bargain with their subject populations, and Norway is a full liberal democracy. And neither does resource extraction in itself guarantee democracy. While democratization has occurred in some countries around the world, it has usually developed as an unintended by-product of extraction.

But grudging consent is not a sufficient condition for democracy. And yet—perhaps seemingly paradoxically—the two authoritarian states might actually be better placed to embark on a path toward democracy than the rentier-state United Arab Emirates.

Chapter 1 introduces the concepts employed in this book. States are not created at a single specific instant and do not remain static thereafter. They change, adapting to different circumstances. States have to continually balance the three basic functions of security, welfare, and representation; they need resources and legitimacy to do so, and taxation is a key element in this. However, in the Middle East states have relied not on taxation to accumulate capital but rather on rents. The interplay of rentierism with traditional patterns of authority (tribal, sectarian and religious) and the means of exercising violence (internally and externally) has thereby largely influenced the process of state making.

Chapter 2 looks at the history of the Iraqi state since its creation in the aftermath of World War I. Iraq has been one of the most warlike states in the Middle East: it was engaged in the 1948 War with Israel, the Six-Day War (June War) of 1967 with Israel, the Yom Kippur War of 1973 with Israel, the Iran-Iraq War (1980–88), the First and Second Gulf Wars (1990–91 and 2003), and the subsequent insurgency (since 2003). The state that emerged was defined by personalized rule, informal relations, and an abundance of oil revenues. These three elements were inherently linked as the abundance of oil revenues and the distributive capacities of the state allowed for political rule to be personalized and based on patronage networks. Much of independent Iraq's history of state making (1958–80) followed the rentier-state paradigm until the onset of the Iran-Iraq War in 1980. This started a new era in the state's history that ultimately led to state failure and collapse: initial war making (the Iran-Iraq War) led to overstretching of state capacity, and the ensuing fiscal crisis led to a further weakening of the state and pushed the regime into bellicosity (the annexation of oil-rich Kuwait in order to shore up Iraq's rentier resources). The concerted military action by the international community and the subsequent regime of United Nations sanctions left the Iraqi state crippled. Having lost the First Gulf War to the United States–led multinational force, the government of Saddam

Hussein was hamstrung by multiple international sanctions and as such could exercise only limited domestic sovereignty. The weakened Iraqi state—a fragile state *par excellence*—had to re-create new forms of legitimacy by resorting to Iraqi nationalism based on tribal affinities and the Islamic religion in order to counter the persistent surveillance by and encroachment of powerful external adversaries. The bellicose public discourse proved counterproductive, as Iraq's supposed military capacity was one of the reasons for the violent regime change in 2003 and the total collapse of the state in the aftermath of the invasion. In terms of the argument of the book, this chapter demonstrates that the combination of rentierism and war making proves particularly deadly to states, as abundance of revenues allows for an unsustainable degree of militarization which is not matched by the institutional strength of the state. Based on an overestimation of military strength, the use of war making in this context is not conducive to state making but rather serves as a destructive force. Therefore, where military capacity is paid for by rulers' rents, state making has effects almost opposite to those of the ruler-subject struggles that characterized early modern Europe. This is one of the major contributions of the book and to our general understanding of state making in rentier states.

Chapter 3 looks at a second war-making state in the region. Jordan, like Iraq, has been engaged in war making since independence. It was involved in the 1948 War with Israel, the Six-Day War (June War) of 1967 with Israel, the military campaign against the PLO and Syria in September 1970, and the Yom Kippur War of 1973 with Israel.[5] From a "war-makes-states" perspective one would again expect the emergence of a strong state. However, the opposite is the case: Jordan shows clear elements of institutional weakness in the domains of representation and welfare, very similarly to Iraq prior to the invasion of Kuwait in 1990. While Jordan has managed to avoid state failure as occurred in Iraq, Jordan is still characterized by weakness. Consequently, Jordan constitutes an intriguing case for explaining state survival in the face of fragility. For much of Jordan's history the state has been in real danger of being wiped off the map—there was no shortage of attempts to incorporate the Hashemite Kingdom into other sovereign states. Yet the Jordanian monarchy has proven to be one of the most resilient in the

Middle East, and the threat of state extinction no longer exists. Contributing to Jordan's survival have been the availability of rents, the evolution of a cohesive civilian and military elite motivated by self-interest in preserving their political patrimony, the loyalty of the armed forces and the domestic security establishment, and the consistent interest of external powers in Jordan's continued stability. All this has been facilitated by financial resources available to Jordan's rulers through foreign rents. Rentierism has thereby contributed to the survival of the Jordanian state in that it allowed generous welfare allocation to key social groups and a high degree of militarization which has strengthened the military establishment. A pure logic of war making and state making cannot explain the longevity of the Jordanian state, as it is both weak and surviving. Rather, this case shows how semi-rentier states broadly follow the path of state making set by oil-rich states. It thus adds to the general argument of the book as it shows how the impact of rentierism can also be felt through the abundance of foreign rents and not just oil rents.

Chapter 4 deals with the history of state making without war making. The chapter looks at the small oil states of the Gulf region and includes a detailed study of the United Arab Emirates. It is clear how oil rents played a crucial role in the emergence of the modern United Arab Emirates. Oil discoveries after World War II first put the United Arab Emirates and its oil-producing neighbors on the international map and served as a bridge for contacts with the rest of the world. Territorial control of the tribal hinterland, the establishment of a state administration, and the fixing of land and sea boundaries became important issues. Since then, oil wealth has enabled the creation of infrastructure and ongoing development, as well as the creation of an extensive state apparatus. Oil revenues thereby consolidated state structures in the absence of war making. The United Arab Emirates embarked on economic diversification during the oil-boom years of the 1970s and set in place a policy of resource and capital acquisition based on attracting foreign direct investment. In this way a sustainable rentier structure was created. War making was never employed as a strategy of state making. Welfare provision in the United Arab Emirates has today become sustainable enough that even during periods of declining natural resources (as in the case of Dubai) or during fiscal crisis (as in the 1980s or 2007), the state is able to fulfill its welfare commitments. In creating a sustainable rentier structure, the United Arab Emirates managed to break the linkage between declining resources and rising demand for political participation. The United Arab Emirates handled oil wealth conducive to state making. In terms of the argument of the book, the United Arab Emirates demonstrates that in the absence of war making, states can create sustainable structures and embedded authority. However, this strategy must be linked with the expansion of self-generated domestic resource extraction in order to produce lasting political change as well as effective and accountable governance in the post-rentier era.

Finally, chapter 5 reviews the empirical and theoretical findings. Two conclusions emerge from the case studies. First, rentierism serves as an obstacle to the formation of strong and legitimate states, since stability rests on a social contract by means of which consent is bought via material welfare. Second—an indeed more novel point—rentierism not only inhibits the emergence of embedded domestic authority structures and empirical sovereignty, but it also acts against the disappearance of weak and fragile states. Were it not for the availability of external rents, many weak states such as Jordan, the United Arab Emirates, and Iraq would probably have succumbed to state failure, even while maintaining a legal façade of quasi-statehood. In Iraq, state failure did indeed occur. The rentier state was broken and state making came to a (temporary) halt in 2003. Since then it has resumed, gradually and with difficulty. In theoretical terms there is a need to extend the Tillyan argument of state making through military competition. Just as war making has historically produced strong states in Europe, it has also destroyed weak states that were not capable enough to survive alongside stronger states; the history of Venice, Brabant, Flanders, Savoy and other formerly sovereign entities in Europe testifies to this. Following this competitive logic, contemporary rentier states (weak, but surviving) must be distinguished from collapsed states, where institutional order breaks down and the situation resembles a war of all against all.

The book concludes by offering insights into post-conflict peace building and state reconstruction policies. It argues that an awareness and knowledge of the factors underlying state-making processes in a different historical and cultural environment have important consequences for ongoing humanitarian projects undertaken by the international community. Without taking the historic, social and political realities of the Arab region into account, these projects cannot succeed, as is illustrated by the difficult current process of state reconstruction in Iraq and Afghanistan.

1

Understanding State Making

No one can run a state without social arrangements that produce and reproduce resources supporting administration, political control, and patronage.

Charles Tilly, "Extraction and democracy"

Making states work is a complex and often arduous task. The requirements are best captured in terms of the three core functions of any modern state: security, welfare, and representation. These three substantial components of state making are sometimes mutually reinforcing and at other times stand in the way of each others' fulfillment.[1] Security stands apart in that it is a precondition for both welfare and representation:

> The value of security comprises the protection of physical existence against internal and external threats. In its internal dimension it borders on the domain of rule in which opportunities for exercising freedom and for political participation are allocated among individuals. These secure the preservation of the physical existence of the individual and serve its advancement [respectively]. With regard to material needs, the latter is provided for in the domain of economic well-being, by means of the allocation of economic gains as well as opportunities for achieving such gains. (Czempiel 1981: 198)

With regard to welfare, it can be noted that an increase in welfare reduces conflict externally and yields the resources necessary to provide security within the state. Furthermore, such an increase boosts the capacity for and propensity to political participation (Lipset 1959; Putnam

1993), prolongs the life expectancy of democracies (Przeworski et al. 2000), and thus ultimately affects the representation function of states. While there might be nuanced disagreement as to whether representation is adequately fulfilled only in liberal democracies or also within other political systems, the real nexus lies in how individual rights, civil rights, citizenship laws, and minority rights are guaranteed within a state. According to this reading, representation allows for long-term peaceful external relations and domestically for the nonviolent resolution of conflicts (Brown, Lynn-Jones, and Miller 1996). Furthermore, representation contributes to optimal solutions to redistribution problems within society and the state (Boix 2003). In its relation to welfare, adequate representation promotes economic growth and social justice (Barro 1997: 49–87; Przeworski et al. 2000), attracts more foreign direct investment (FDI), and makes aid more effective (Jensen 2003; Kosack 2003).

*　*　*

The third function of the modern state is to provide representation and legitimacy. The notion that rulers should be legitimate in the eyes of their subjects is quite an old one—it can be traced back to at least the Middle Ages (Skinner 1989; Van Creveld 1999). However, the idea that the modern state ought to legitimately represent the ensemble of its subjects is relatively new, dating to the eighteenth and early nineteenth centuries. Not surprisingly, there is little consensus over exactly what, in concrete terms, makes a state legitimate or representative. Nationalism and democracy (the latter understood to include the rule of law and respect for basic political human rights) are often proposed as the two most important means by which these functions of representation and legitimacy are realized. In its strictest sense, of course, legitimacy means "compliance with law" (Wilson 1988). In a broader sense the meaning of the word "legitimacy" is not restricted to that which is sanctioned by law. This common use of the word implies that an action is just or right irrespective of its legality and thus describes the subjective understanding of actors as to what is deemed politically legitimate. Democracy is defined here as a political system that meets three conditions, namely: meaningful and extensive competition for all effective positions of government power at regular intervals and excluding the use of force; highly inclusive political participation in the selection of leaders and policies, at least through regular and fair elections, such that no major social group is excluded; and a level of civil and political liberties sufficient to ensure the integrity of political competition and participation (Linz, Diamond, and Lipset 1988). Authoritarian states, on the other hand, are political systems that allow for only limited political pluralism, lack extensive or intensive political mobilization, and are characterized by having a leader or small group that effectively rules (Linz 1975). Focusing on the representative functions of states leads to a focus on nation-building, incorporation of social groups into welfare mechanisms, and the construction of embedded authority structures. Failure to construct the latter is a failure by the state to adequately represent its people. Legitimacy of rulers and of political rule is central.

Functions of the State

States do not come into existence at a specific moment and then remain static. They change and adapt to different circumstances. In that sense, they reform and transform in a constant process that requires balancing of the three basic state functions. Occasionally, states also deform, which leads to state failure. This occurs when war making acts as a destructive force. Wars can have formative and organizing effects, as in early modern Europe, but also disintegrative or reformative effects, as in the Middle East. Wars sometimes diminish state power and lead states into failure to fulfill basic functions. The state may even dwindle to produce institutional state collapse—a rare phenomenon in the current international state system—or may reform and transform. States may be weak, grow stronger, and then over time weaken again. Formation is a permanent process with multiple effects along the way that range from functional state failure to state reformation to occasional state collapse as well as to lasting weak state structures.

States which undergo reformation possess proper state institutions and display most of the functions of the modern state (usually one or two out of the three functions discussed above). They are functioning entities, and their cases must be distinguished from those of state failure or collapse. Yet they are also distinct from the states that emerged in Western Europe (Sørensen 2001; Clapham 1998). However, much scholarship has taken Max Weber's ideal type, which sees the state as a given, and has failed to deal with forms of statehood.[2] With Weber's ideal-type state as a starting point, scholars can conceptualize and measure variation in states only in comparison with the ideal type and are thus limited by a narrow focus in their analysis of state making and of those states which fall short of this ideal. State building is measured against not what states are, but what they should be. But perhaps the "ideal state" is not the rule but the exception in the world. The "natural" state might not monopolize legitimate violence, but instead broker civil peace in exchange for the rights to extract rents (North, Wallis, and Weingast 2009; Snyder 2010). In that sense, the weak and fragile states of the Middle East, such as Iraq and Jordan, look more like the rule than the exception.

*   *   *

Empirically, one can observe tremendous variations among states in terms of actual state capacity, societal control, mobilization, and the distribution of resources. The functioning nature of many states in the non-European world points to the existence of several forms of statehood, understood in terms of functions and not international law. The degree of difference of these functioning states compared with many European states (and the Weberian ideal type) often relates to the proper role of state institutions, where the basic functions of the modern state are often fulfilled by non-state actors and where state institutions are deliberately or accidentally bypassed. In the Middle East this is highlighted by the informal character of politics (Sharabi 1988) and the existence of powerful alternative loyalties other than to the state (tribal, sectarian or religious).

Consequently, different evolutionary pathways to state making can be observed. Some of these pathways produce institutionally strong and legitimate states. The states that emerged in early modern Europe are cases in point. Other pathways are less conducive to state making and may lead to weak and fragile states, as the case of Jordan and Iraq demonstrates. Finally, there are pathways to state making which are

Table 1.1. Degrees of statehood: Transformation of the state

	Strong state (Weberian ideal type)	Reformed state (industrialized post-welfare state)	Rentier state (allocation state)	Weak state (non-Western state)	Failed state (functional and institutional failure)
Security function	×	×	×	×	—
Welfare function	×	—	×	—	—
Representation function	×	×	—	—	—

Source: Adapted from Schwarz 2008a.

distinct from the European experience, but which nevertheless lead to the main functions of modern states being fulfilled. The rentier states of the Gulf such as the United Arab Emirates are cases in point: these states have developed features of modern statehood and yet depend for their internal functioning on different conjectures from those of Western European states, relating to factors including the role of institutions, revenues, and personal relations.

Table 1.1 summarizes the different concepts employed in this book. State making should be seen as a continuum on the horizontal line of the table. The distinction between strong state, reformed state, rentier state, weak state, and failed state follows a functional understanding of the state. Such an understanding measures statehood against the fulfillment of core functions, including the provision of internal and external security, the provision of welfare and wealth, and the provision of a certain level of representation. The types of statehood mentioned below are inductively obtained, and different combinations of the core functions of states are conceivable, giving rise to different types of statehood.

Transformation of the state denotes the process through which a renegotiation of state functions occurs: the term describes changes in the public conception of what it means for the state to fulfill its core functions. One example would be a shift away from a strong state to a reformed state. This occurred in many European states during the 1990s and the first decade of the twenty-first century, when the state withdrew from its welfare function and citizens were asked to take on more private responsibility in that domain. Another example would be a shift away from a rentier state that was initially able to fully distribute welfare benefits to its citizens but, due to a fiscal crisis, has to reduce its welfare function. Many Arab states in the late 1980s fit this pattern of a rentier state under fiscal constraint. They had to adjust their welfare functions, re-negotiate the classic formula of "no taxation, no representation," and ultimately widen their political legitimacy, thereby affecting the representation function of the state. Non-state groups, mainly Islamists, filled the gap and gained legitimacy by providing socioeconomic services that the state could no longer provide, and in this way challenged the state. Such was the case in Algeria, where the Islamic Salvation Front (Front Islamique du Salut, FIS) took over many social services abandoned by the state, and violently challenged the state (Chhibber 1996). Such was also the case in Yemen, where a withdrawal of state-provided welfare led to civil war (1994) and rebellion in the north (since 2004).

Focusing on a functional understanding of statehood allows us to highlight cases where Arab states are strong (in the security function and, in times of abundant rents, in the welfare function) and where they are weak (in the representation function and, in times of fiscal crisis, in the welfare function). The transition from one form to the other and the renegotiation of state-society relations risks bringing about violent and turbulent transitions. Hence Arab regimes have to balance external and internal security threats (David 1991; Gause 1994).

State Making in a Globalized World

Charles Tilly's approach to state making provides an interesting and rich kaleidoscope of questions. His account, as well as those studies on state making in the developing world that follow the same logic, assume a teleological path to state making, one which runs from war making to extraction and repression to state making. This narrow teleological focus, as well as the emphasis on a single major factor determining state making (i.e., war making and its institutional consequences) poses problems for a general account of state making, not only in the difficulty it has in accounting for variations in state building across early modern Europe, but also with regard to alternative factors driving state building in other parts of the world.[3]

Tilly has been quite cautious about the extent to which his approach to state building might provide lessons that could be generalized to more recent periods and other regions. In *Coercion, Capital and European States,* he questioned the existence of a teleological path of state making and tried to provide an answer that accounted for the "great variations over time and space in the kinds of states that have prevailed in Europe since AD 990" (Tilly 1990: 32). He described three different short-term variations in state-building trajectories: coercive-intensive (examples included Russia, Hungary, Serbia, Sweden, and Brandenburg-Prussia), capital-intensive (Venice, Genoa, and the Dutch Republic) and capitalized-coercive (France and England). Thus it seems he went beyond a teleological approach to state building. However, while conceding to short-term variations, he concluded that only those states would survive that emulated the successful practices of the leading (capitalized-coercive) states and that over time all existing states converged on a single path:

> Driven by the pressures of international competition (especially by war and preparation for war) all three paths eventually converged on concentrations of capital and coercion . . . From the seventeenth century onwards the capitalized coercion form proved more effective in war, and therefore provided a compelling model for states that had originated in other combinations of coercion and capital. (Tilly 1990: 31)

For, while capital-intensive structures held their own for centuries "until the sheer scale of war with nationally recruited armies and navies overwhelmed their efficient but compact military power" (ibid.: 151), they eventually had to give in to larger and more industrialized states, which were able to impose their supremacy within the international system due to the massive costs of war (ibid.: 63–66, 187–91). Only those states that adapted successfully to the international military competition survived, while maladaptive states disappeared. Thus, while Tilly accounted for different state-building trajectories in the short run, he argued that in the long run it was the state's ability to adapt to a single logic—that of international military competition—that accounted for the final outcome of state building, the capitalized-coercive nation-state.

Two distinct phases of state building are identified by Tilly. The first phase is covered in his seminal work *The Formation of National States in Western Europe* (1975) as well as his article "War making and state making as organized crime" (1985). The later phase is covered in his *Coercion, Capital and European States* (1990). The principal limitation of his early work and its adaptations to the Third World is, as we argued above, that it presents a teleological path to state building (one which runs from war to extraction and repression to state building). Supposedly, all European states historically followed this path, and all contemporary states are to follow it in order to achieve empirical sovereignty. However, this is not the case, as there are many variations in state building processes—in early modern Europe and in the contemporary Third World and the Middle East. The central aim of *Coercion, Capital and European States* was therefore to account for precisely these variations in state building. For this purpose the dual logic of capital and coercion was introduced. In the end Tilly did not provide a more complex account of different paths to state building, but reproduced a state building logic in conformity with the neo-realist logic of anarchy and international military competition between states.

*   *   *

I join Tilly in arguing that different pathways to state making exist, not only in the short run but also in the long run. In the Middle East we find a specific pathway: rentier states have large amounts of revenue at their disposal, which reduces their need to levy taxes from their citizens and to generate domestic resources. This diminished need for domestic capital in turn impedes the emergence of a strong state that legitimately represents its citizens. But it also allows state institutions to provide welfare through patronage channels and distribution policies.

This pathway then leads to a weakness of the state in terms of its ability to represent all citizens equally and to allocate wealth to its clients and followers. Taken together, the level of rentierism contributes to the emergence of institutionally weak states that are sustainable enough to survive. Jordan provides a good illustration of this.

The Middle East shows another interesting aspect with regard to variations in the pathway of state making. While it is implicit in most theories of international relations and state building that similar combinations of factors will produce similar results (and hence provide similar explanations), this overlooks the possibility that similar events or developments might have not only varying but even opposite effects in different spatial and historical contexts. In some cases, war making and international military competition have led to the weakening of state structures and indeed state failure, as in Iraq (see the following chapter). Other examples of state failure in the wider Middle Eastern region include Algeria, Lebanon, Somalia, Sudan, Yemen, and now Libya, and in fact one might expect others to follow, given the weakness and fragility of states in the region. A refinement of Tilly's approach to state making needs thus to ask under which conditions war making leads to the weakening of state structures and to state failure.

A third refinement for understanding of state making concerns an emphasis on more complex notions of history, spatial and cultural context, and the possibility of seeing beyond international military competition as the driving force of state building. In particular, the growing importance of economic globalization and the apparent restraints this imposes on the behavior of states seems to provide a quite different context of state building compared with that in early modern Europe, some 600 years earlier. War making has changed in its nature, not only with technological innovations over the centuries (Kaldor 1999; Van Creveld 1991), but also with regard to its meaning and its regularity (Brown, Lynn-Jones, and Miller 1996). Indeed, a key assumption in the Tillyan model of state building is that resources, once extracted from society, are used by state elites either to wage wars or to prepare effectively for the eventuality of war. In a globalized world, states no longer primarily seek to wage war, but compete with other states in terms of economic growth and economic development. The new driving engine has become globalization and resistance to it (Schwarz 2008b). States no longer play the key role in resource extraction; private actors are increasingly central to understanding developing countries. While, at the beginning of the 1990s, around 75 percent of all international capital transfers still involved states, this proportion has since declined to less than 25 percent (Strange 1996). States are clearly in retreat and are more and more dependent on private actors; they have to acquire loans on the private market and are dependent on the willingness of firms and affluent citizens to pay taxes in their home country.[4] Indeed, globalization has rendered taxation and resource extraction more difficult as firms can threaten to relocate their production or make their investments elsewhere if costs are too high. States have thus partly lost their capacity to sanction private actors. International financial regulations are today characterized by the absence of governance, and private actors, creditors, foreign investors, and wealthy citizens are left uncontrolled by a weakened state authority (Leander 2001: 125). One may even go so far as to argue that private actors have developed a capacity to sanction states, or at least threaten to do so. All these points serve to support the argument that historical change needs to be taken into account when analyzing such complex phenomena as state building. While Tilly's approach to state building does not account for historical change as such, one may claim that states generally and across the centuries pursue power. In the Middle Ages and the early modern period this occurred through war; in today's globalized world it occurs through economic growth and development. The fundamental mechanism of state building, based on resource extraction, the generation of welfare and institutional growth, remains a valid point of reference.

Different pathways to state making depend not only on divergent historical settings, but also on different spatial contexts. With particular reference to the Middle East, a focus on societal and cultural understandings and how they determine different contexts in which such factors as war making, extraction, repression, and state institutions operate, is paramount. Far from assuming culturalist determinism, and rather in line with Max Weber, I see people's behavior as being linked to interests and motives and these in turn as being expressed in terms of values and culture. The incorporation of culture into the analysis of state-building processes should not be seen as a factor by itself, but rather as a result of material conditions (identities being forged by states) and as the context in which state building occurs. State building in present-day developing countries differs from the historical development of the states in Western Europe during the early modern period (given the different spatial setting) and cannot be fully understood without reference to the cultural and historic context within which certain factors operate. The limitations of approaches which do not account for differences in history and space are most obvious in the analysis of state making in the Third World (Ayoob 1996). Consequently, a refinement of our understanding of state making ought to include a critical awareness of different historical contexts (the early modern era in contrast to today's globalized world) and different spatial contexts (the cultural background of Middle Eastern societies in contrast to Western Europe). While it is true that predatory states are today somewhat marginal in the world's geography, examples do still exist. Many of these contemporary predatory states are situated precisely in the Middle East and thus raise a warning against letting go of Tilly's approach to state building completely. The latter's usefulness lies exactly in the fact that it highlights the importance of institutions of organized violence for state building. While only detailed empirical analyses can show to what degree war making and international military competition influenced state building, the approach should not be discarded from the outset.

Taxation, Oil Revenues, and State Weakness in the Middle East

Resource extraction is a key feature in the process of building viable states. State capacity can be empirically evaluated through the level of tax revenues accrued by the state (domestic revenue extraction). State strength is thus infrastructural power, namely the capacity of the state to actually penetrate civil society and to implement logistically political decisions throughout the realm (Mann 1993). State capacity means the extent to which interventions of state agents in existing non-state resources, activities, and interpersonal connections alter existing distributions of those resources across the population (Tilly 2007a). It can also be evaluated through revenue accumulation, namely the ratio of external rents to state revenues (external revenue accumulation). This is particularly pronounced in oil states that do not have to rely on domestic resource extraction. They enjoy a degree of autonomy from society due to the availability of abundant natural resources. Hence they display a particular pathway to state building that by and large defies the European pathway: oil abundance created structures of authority that were autonomous of societal demands and did not rely on consent achieved through domestic taxation. State building was not accompanied by political accountability, transparency, or what Tilly has termed the "civilianization of government and domestic politics" (Tilly 1990: 206).

Looking at domestic revenue extraction, there are only a handful of states in the Middle East that have this capacity. The ratio of tax revenues to government revenues shows that only Tunisia, Morocco, and Israel come close to the average OECD (Organisation for Economic Co-operation and Development) level, where the percentage of direct taxes as a proportion of state revenues usually stands at around 40 percent and total taxes amount to well over 90 percent of state revenues.[5] For Morocco the percentage of direct taxes on state revenues amounted to 25–30 percent for 1999–2003 and, if indirect taxes are included, to 70–75 percent on average.[6] In Tunisia the percentage of direct taxes for the same period was at a similar level—around 25 percent. Adding indirect taxes brings the amount to more than 85 percent in Tunisia and over a long period consistently more than 80 percent.[7] In Israel the proportion for direct taxes is around 40 percent, and if indirect taxes are added the figure is around 80 percent.

Table 1.2 shows that of all the Arab states, Tunisia comes closest to the level of OECD states in terms of taxation. Tunisia is a strong state fully in the Weberian sense, but at the same time was until recently one of the most repressive and authoritarian states in the Middle East. Tunisia was a paradigm case for an Arab state that was economically liberal but politically aggressive (see Ayubi 1995). Events in 2011 and the change of regime have made Tunisia now a paradigm case for

Table 1.2. OECD and selected Middle Eastern states compared (percentage of taxes of state revenues)

	1999	2000	2001	2002	2003	2004
MOROCCO						
Direct taxes	25	25[a]	23	30	31	—
Total taxes	76	76	70	88	84	—
TUNISIA						
Direct taxes	23	23	26	26	28	25
Total taxes	85	83	88	82	85	76
ISRAEL						
Direct taxes	—	46	48	41	41	41
Total taxes	—	79	82	76	77	79
GERMANY (OECD)						
Direct taxes	38	39	38	38	38	—
Total taxes	92	92[b]	92	92	92	93
NETHERLANDS (OECD)						
Direct taxes	—	42	40	40	39	39
Total taxes	—	93	93	94	94	94

Source: Author's calculations (Schwarz 2008a: 605).

Notes: a. In Morocco the fiscal year extended from July to June in 1999 and since 2001 extends from January to December. The period of July-December 2000 was a transitional accounting period between fiscal years.

b. Data excluding receipts from auction of Universal Mobile Telecommunications System mobile phone licenses of EUR 50.85 bn.

democratization. A regional perspective on the taxation effort in the Arab Middle East provides an even clearer picture. Taxation, measured as a percentage of total state revenues, gives an appreciation of a state's infrastructural power (or lack thereof) and its ability (or inability) to actively seek revenues on desired policies.

Table 1.3 shows how oil rentier states (Algeria, Bahrain, Kuwait, Oman, the United Arab Emirates [UAE]) tax considerably lower than non-oil states.[8] Syria, Palestine, and Yemen stand apart as rentier states despite apparent differences from the oil-exporting countries of the Gulf. Yemen and Syria possess natural resources but have comparatively small populations. This increases the ratio of state revenues to

Table 1.3. Tax revenues in the Arab Middle East (as percentage of state revenues)

	1993	1994	1995	1996	1997	1998	1999
Algeria	42	41	39	35	34	43	33
Bahrain	—	—	—	—	—	—	—
Egypt	59	60	62	63	63	65	66
Iraq	n/a	n/a	n/a	n/a	n/a	n/a	n/a
Jordan	46	47	45	49	49	50	55
Kuwait	4	3	3	2	3	4	2
Lebanon	65	74	69	81	77	70	68
Libya	n/a	n/a	n/a	n/a	n/a	n/a	n/a
Morocco	n/a	69	73	70	85	81	76
Oman	n/a	n/a	n/a	n/a	n/a	n/a	n/a
Palestine	—	—	—	26	27	26	26
Qatar	—	—	—	—	—	—	—
Saudi Arabia	7	8	6	6	5	9	8
Syria	24	28	30	37	38	32	32
Tunisia	80	81	82	79	81	78	85
UAE	16	13	17	19	15	18	13
Yemen	57	59	48	23	25	35	25

Source: Author's calculations (adapted from Schwarz 2008a: 606).

Note: Author's calculations based on Economist Intelligence Unit (various years, various countries); Bahrain 2006; IMF, 2004a, 2004b; Kuwait (various years); Lebanon 1994, 2010; Oman 2000, 2001, 2002, 2003, 2005, 2007, 2008; Qatar 2005; Saudi Arabia 1998, 2005; Tunisia 1999; UAE 1999; UAE Central Bank (various years); the figures for Egypt are from Richter 2004 and Economist Intelligence Unit 2007b and 2008c. Only those states that list tax revenues as a separate item in public finances have been included here (n/a = no numbers available).

number of beneficiaries of rent distribution. Thus, states such as Yemen and Syria increase the distribution effect of rents and can be considered rentier or distributive states.[9] In that sense Palestine is also a rentier state, because only a small portion of state revenues comes from taxation and a much larger portion come from rents (Brynen 2000), and because those taxes that are collected are levied by the Israeli authorities and then transferred to the Palestinian Authority.[10] Non-oil states differ between those that rely heavily on taxation (Tunisia, Morocco, Lebanon) and those that rely on both taxation and external rents (Jordan and Egypt). Only in those states that rely solely on taxation (Tu-

2000	2001	2002	2003	2004	2005	2006
22	27	24	24	28	21	20
—	—	—	—	—	—	—
66	59	65	66	68	65	63
n/a	n/a	n/a	n/a	1	1	1
57	62	57	65	67	69	67
1	2	2	3	3	15	9
61	64	68	68	69	66	60
n/a	n/a	n/a	n/a	n/a	n/a	n/a
76	70	88	84	83	84	n/a
7	5	5	5	6	7	7
26	26	24	37	20	19	n/a
—	—	—	—	—	—	—
5	n/a	n/a	n/a	n/a	n/a	n/a
31	36	54	51	52	50	44
83	88	82	85	83	85	80
10	9	12	9	10	5	4
18	20	22	23	22	21	18

nisia, Morocco, and Lebanon) is the state's infrastructural power well established.

This suggests two general trends within the Middle East and with regard to rentierism: oil-exporting states (pure rentier states) have had the privilege not to have to tax their populations, while other states have relied on a mixture of rents and taxation for their state revenues. However, the latter states (Jordan, Egypt) have relied not on direct taxation, but on indirect means of levying resources (such as tariffs, sales tax, or licensing) in order to cover structural weaknesses.[11] Where taxation did occur, it was mainly levied on state-owned companies (mainly in the oil industry) and foreign companies. In other words, the state levied taxes from itself and from foreigners and not from society.

With respect to the structure of the tax system in the Arab world, there are further problems beyond the general low level of taxation: taxes are levied mainly in an indirect manner; income-tax revenues are negligible and tax evasion is rampant. This has obvious consequences for state making. All these elements point toward the weakness of states in the Middle East (United Nations Development Programme 2005: 153). Autocratic governments are generally ineffective at raising direct taxes, since collection of taxes requires widespread voluntary compliance by citizens and an efficient and legitimate bureaucracy (Fauvelle-Aymar 1999: 406). The evidence presented above confirms that the more a state relies on direct measures of taxation, the more the collection of taxes depends on an efficient bureaucracy and voluntary compliance. In the absence of voluntary compliance, mainly linked to a lack of legitimacy, states have to rely on indirect measures to accrue the necessary revenues. This trend has consequences for state-making dynamics: a focus on only the war-making strategies of a country is insufficient, as is set out in greater detail in the following chapters analyzing two war-making states, Iraq and Jordan, as well as in contrast the state-making trajectory in the United Arab Emirates. All three states analyzed in this book fall short of theoretical expectations linked to the "war-makes-states" theory.

2

Iraq

From Rentier State to Failed State

War at best leaves states where they are and at worst speeds up their unraveling. It therefore seems particularly unwise to follow the recommendations of those who advocate giving war a chance in building states.

Anna Leander, "Wars and the unmaking of states"

Iraq has been one of the most war-prone states in the Middle East. It was engaged in the 1948 War with Israel, the 1967 Six-Day War (June War) with Israel, the 1973 Yom Kippur War with Israel, the 1980–88 Iran-Iraq War, the First and Second Gulf Wars (1990–91 and 2003), and after the latter war, the insurgency (since 2003). Contrary to the war-makes-states theory, Iraq's war making has not strengthened the state; it has rather led to its demise. It is argued in this chapter that the combination of war making and rentierism proves to be particularly deadly to states, as this produces state failure and potentially the breakdown of the rentier state. In Iraq, the abundance of revenues allowed for an unsustainable degree of militarization, which was not matched by institutional strength of the state. War making based on an overestimation of military strength was not conducive to state making, but rather acted as a destructive force. This chapter highlights how collective violence and "the cumulative impact of war" (Owen 2000) weakened the state of Iraq in the 1980s and led to its failure. By 2003 Iraq was already a failed state that did not fulfill its functions and provide public goods to its populace. The U.S.-led invasion in 2003 further contributed to the collapse of state institutions in the aftermath of the earlier outside intervention.[1]

War and State Making in Iraq

The Iraqi state was created in 1921 under British mandate. Iraq's history of state making has followed the same path as many other developing states in the struggle against a major foreign power and the attempt to create modern state institutions through war. The modern state that eventually emerged was defined by personalized rule, informal relations and abundance of oil revenues. These three elements were inherently linked as the abundance of oil revenues and the distributive capacities of the state allowed for political rule to be personalized and based on patronage networks. Much of Iraq's modern history (1958–80) followed the rentier state paradigm until the onset of the Iran-Iraq War in 1980; at this time a new era of the state's history began that was characterized by the unmaking of the state. The disposition of the belligerent Iraqi rentier state to war making was marked by an overestimation of its military strength, and proved catastrophic.

*   *   *

The history of Iraq since its creation in 1921 demonstrates both the destructive and the constructive powers of war making. Two key institutions were founded in the years following the end of World War I: the local Arab administration under British mandate, and the Iraqi army (Luizard 1994: 268). The local Arab administration set about the task of building a new state. It focused primarily on education as a way of creating a national identity. These efforts created a new urban-based middle class which was heavily influenced by nationalistic indoctrination, militaristic ceremonial, regional politics, and the struggle against the French in Syria; political activism translated into violent protests in 1928, and again in the 1930s and during World War II. The new middle class found employment in the state administration either as civilians (teachers, officials, engineers) or in the military (Batatu 1978: 319; Eppel 1998: 237). Representation of the middle classes in parliament increased from around 20 percent in 1933–37 to around 35 percent in the decade 1943–53 (Eppel 1998: 243). Alongside this increased influence, opposition grew from the old landowners and tribal leaders, who were particularly hostile to the new urban elite.

The other key institution of the new Iraqi state, the military, was initially created only as the Iraq Levies, with the task of garrisoning Royal Air Force bases. However, the threat of war with Turkey forced the British to expand Iraq's indigenous military forces (Pollack 2002). The Iraqi military had Arab officers, who had served in the Ottoman army but deserted during World War I (during the 1916 Arab Revolt). The number of such officers at the time is estimated at between 400 and 600 (Hemphill 1979: 98). A sense of Arabness and Arab nationalism had first started to emerge in the Ottoman army following the Young Turks' Revolution of 1908. The Arab officers remodeled themselves on the nationalism of the Young Turks and the latter's policy of Turkification. Many ex-Ottoman officers came to influence both Iraqi politics and the military. Between 1922 and 1932 nine out of 14 Iraqi prime ministers were ex-Ottoman officers (among them Nuri as-Saʿid, Jaʿfar al-ʿAskari, and Yasin al-Hashimi), as were 32 out of 56 cabinet ministers (ibid.: 91–92).

The role of these Arab officers was not clear from the outset. Indeed, the very establishment of the Iraqi army in 1921 became a bone of contention. At the Cairo Conference of 1921 the British mandatory power decided to jointly provide the defense forces of the country: the Iraqis would form the regular army and the British would supplement it with Royal Air Force (RAF) units and the British-led Iraq Levies. This dual plan would gradually evolve so that eventually the defense of Iraq would lie in the hands of its own people, and that the new Iraqi state would allocate no less than 25 percent of its revenues to defensive purposes (ibid.: 94). In reality, however, British objections to an Iraqi army run entirely by Iraqis became paramount, and the British government was hesitant to give more autonomy to an institution which could be used for nationalistic propaganda purposes. Such sentiments were indeed held by many Iraqis at the time and were put forward in writing by many educated Iraqis (Al-Sabbagh 1956). In June 1927, Prime Minister Jaʿfar al-ʿAskari introduced a conscription bill into the Iraqi parliament; Britain objected to it on the grounds that it was too costly and that it would encounter tribal opposition. The British won out regarding the contending visions of the role and scope of the new Iraqi army: the bill was withdrawn, the Cabinet resigned, and the army's formation followed the British dual plan as proposed in 1921.

By 1929 the process of state making had nevertheless advanced. The Iraqi army had been trained sufficiently to be able to defend Iraq's borders and provide internal order, with the support of the RAF, according to a League of Nations report on the administration of Iraq for 1928. The Iraqi army had indeed expanded greatly since its establishment, from 3,500 troops in 1922 to 7,000 in 1927; the troops doubled again between 1932 and 1936, after the conscription bill was finally passed in 1934, and reached 11,500 at independence (Hemphill 1979: 97; Glubb 1983). The officer corps started in 1922 with a complement of around 250 (of the 600 ex-Ottoman officers), and over the ensuing years increased proportionately with the expansion in the number of troops, at a ratio of 24:1 (Hemphill 1979: 98–99). The proportion of ex-Ottoman officers decreased from 70 percent in 1927, to 50 percent in 1932 and eventually 15 percent in 1936 (ibid.: 99). Training of new officers was undertaken at a staff college established in 1927 and via training courses held in India and the United Kingdom. Since military training was based on the British Sandhurst model, the new officer corps represented mainly the wealthy and urban families of Iraq (Sluglett 1976: 273–95). In 1928, only 25 percent of officers came from a tribal background, compared with 75 percent of infantrymen (Hemphill 1979: 99).

The military in Iraq, unlike in neighboring Jordan, ceased to be a refuge for members of tribes and an instrument of social mobility; it became an elite-based institution and could now function as the vehicle of a militant pan-Arab nationalism. Iraq's military produced a mingling of Arab identity, anti-imperialist sentiment, and military organization. This mingling was "captivated by the dream we awakened to see in the Iraqi army, the Arab Prussia, the force able to realize our dreams of establishing a great Arab state which would restore to the Arab nation its past glories and forgotten civilization" (Durra 1969; cited in Hemphill 1979: 101). The Iraqi military perceived itself indeed as state- and nation-builder. In a confidential memorandum of March 1933, King Faisal I of Iraq called the military the "spinal column for nation-forming" (Batatu 1978: 26). The military was employed as a means of promoting Arabization and a sense of nationhood; but at the same time it was vulnerable to pan-Arab ideology. Much as with early modern Europe, this could have resulted in state making. However, given the appeal of pan-Arabism, the Iraqi military was more attentive to regional and international influences than to its role as a state-maker; here also it differed from neighboring Jordan.

In terms of popular representation, state making took place initially against the will of the country's two largest sociocultural groups, the Kurds and the Shi'ites. The censuses of 1920 and 1931 indicate that at that time Shi'ites accounted for roughly 55 percent of the population, Sunni Arabs 22 percent, and Kurds around 14 percent, with the remainder comprising various minorities such as Assyrians, Chaldeans, and Turcomans (Sluglett 1976: 300). State institutions were established in a way that paid little consideration to the heterogeneity of Iraqi society. For example, at no time did Shi'ites play a role in government or state administration in true proportion to their numbers in society; neither did state making in Iraq follow "sectarian solidarity" (Sluglett and Farouk-Sluglett 1978: 86). Only since 2003 has the sectarian logic received greater attention, but it has not facilitated the still-difficult process of state reconstruction.

*   *   *

Violence, and not sectarian solidarity, characterized the process of state making in Iraq: the violent struggle against the British mandatory power, as well as the force employed by the Iraqi army internally—as in the Assyrian affair of 1933 (Hemphill 1979: 105–7). During the summer of 1933 the Iraqi military under Colonel Bakr Sidiqi intervened violently against the Christian Assyrian minority, in what has been termed a "pogrom." The conflict began with a political dispute between the Assyrian spiritual leader Mar Shimun and the government in Baghdad. The Assyrians were seen as a perpetuating symbol of Iraq's disunity (forced upon Iraqis by the mandate power) and an icon of parallel state structure (by 1933 some 4,000 Assyrians had passed through the Iraqi Levies, and were allowed to retain their rifles, thereby creating a miniature parallel army); thus, the military seized the opportunity to impose its monopoly of force. The violence and repression employed against the Assyrians was perceived as a great success for the military and a step toward the establishment of an Arab state in Iraq. Moreover, there were other cases of direct repression against Shiʿites and Kurds—such as in 1923, when the Iraqi government exiled several Shiʿites under the pretext that they were Persians and hence aliens in Iraq (Al-Adhami 1979: 21; Luizard 1994: 268–70).

The difficulties of the path toward state making were further highlighted by the power struggle between King Faisal, the British government, and the anti-British movement. This became particularly pronounced in the run-up to the parliamentary assembly elections in 1922–24 (Al-Adhami 1979: 13–31). In June 1920 the British authorities announced that Sir Percy Cox, later to be High Commissioner for Iraq, would set up an interim president and an elective assembly, to be freely elected by the Iraqi population. By November 1920 a provisional council of state had been installed and the revision of Ottoman electoral law proclaimed. Elections to the assembly took place only in October 1922 and the first stage lasted until January 1923. The tribal revolt in 1920, the restructuring of the Iraqi state as a monarchy under King Faisal in 1921 and the negotiations over the legal nature of the British mandate (the Anglo-Iraqi Treaty of October 1922) left this process in limbo and made the establishment of broad-based representation more difficult. When elections finally took place in 1922 and 1924, political life was not organized along party lines—a fact that would continue to characterize Iraqi political life until after World War II—but remained centered on a few outspoken personalities. In addition to this, the majority of Shiʿite Iraqis abstained from participating in the elections since several fatwas forbidding participation had been issued and were widely disseminated in Iraq (ibid.: 19).

*   *   *

Militant nationalism in the early years of state making, the struggle to establish parliamentary institutions, and acts of outright repression against ethnic minorities demonstrated that Iraq's very creation as a modern state involved several elements that were also characteristic of state formation in early modern Europe: consolidation of the state was aided by violence against the British mandate during the 1920 revolt and the anti-imperial struggle during the 1930s. Although Iraq fell short of strict standards of parliamentary democracy,[2] during this period the country did enjoy a community-based pluralist system based on primordial associations. Claims emerging particularly in the aftermath of the 2003 invasion of Iraq about the absence of any parliamentary life in the modern history of Iraq are unfounded (Dodge 2004). However, a civil society based on conceptions of voluntary choice and individual freedom was missing. Stability was assured by assigning parliamentary seats to tribal sheikhs, religious leaders, and representatives from sectarian and ethnic groups. Political parties, where they existed, were first and foremost a group of persons centered on one or several personalities and united by personal relations and not by common ideology. The modernization and ensuing social transformation of the country slowly undermined this monarchical system. The exodus of Iraqi Jews after 1948 was an initial sign of the changing social order; it allowed Shi'ite merchants to take over and dominate the position vacated by the Jews and gain in social status compared with the Sunnis. The 1952 agreement between the British Iraq Petroleum Company and the Iraqi state was a second sign. This set Iraq on the path toward becoming a rentier state: the country was endowed with considerable natural resources that allowed for large-scale distribution of welfare benefits, but this brought with it a breakdown in the semi-feudal order and the onset of migration to the large cities, particularly Baghdad, with concomitant rapid urbanization. Between 1919 and 1968 the population of Iraq grew almost fourfold, and that of Baghdad eightfold (Al-Din 1970: 11–15; Al-Khafaji 2000: 261). The differences between the provincial life previously enjoyed by the migrants and the new reality of urban Baghdad served to accentuate social antagonisms.

The social and political environment of Iraq during the 1950s was marked by a growing sense of marginality among poorer immigrants, who were attracted to the Iraq Communist Party, and a growing gap between the monarchy and its social base of large landowners and the marginalized masses (Batatu 1978). The 1958 revolution, which overthrew King Faisal II (1935–58) and the Hashemite monarchy, grew out of these social tensions. There were profound changes: the old landowning elite was replaced by a civil-military bureaucracy. This took place via a land reform that set a ceiling on how much land individuals could own, ending the influence of large landholders. In reality, little changed politically, and the new Revolutionary Command Council (RCC) exercised absolute authority (N. Brown 2002: 86). The revolution, despite its avowed goal of bringing about parliamentary democracy, failed to create embedded state institutions. Much remained personal, arbitrary, and factional. Instead of a president, a three-man sovereign council (comprising one Sunni, one Shi'ite, and one Kurd) was set up to lead the country. The first cabinet included four army officers, including the leaders of the revolution, prime minister 'Abd al-Karim Qasim and deputy prime minister 'Abd as-Salam 'Arif. Between July 1958 and February 1963 Qasim was ruling the country alone, but instead of broadening his political and social base through the establishment of permanent state institutions, he ruled with the help of few trusted individuals.

In 1963, the Ba'th party mounted a successful coup against Qasim. The party, led by a Sunni elite under the leadership of 'Arif (1963–66), brought renewed force to the question of Iraqi nationalism and further increased confessional cleavages. 'Arif—who was incidentally a grand-nephew of King Faisal I—became president of Iraq in 1963 and ruled until 1966, when he was killed in a helicopter crash in southern Iraq. He was replaced by his brother 'Abdul Rahman 'Arif, who ruled for only two years.

July 1968 saw another coup, with the Ba'th party ousting 'Abdul Rahman 'Arif. A regime of Ba'th party rule was established and extended into all spheres of life. Party president Ahmad Hasan al-Bakr became state president, prime minister, and army commander-in-chief. While the party did initially give posts to non-party members, it retained a two-thirds majority of all cabinet posts from 1973 onwards and created its own militia, in 1978 numbering some 50,000 men (Yapp 1991: 241). The militia was used for the construction of the state, and violence became a feature of the Iraqi state-making project.

The period of coups saw a sharp increase in military expenditure, from 7 percent of the gross domestic product (GDP) in 1958 to 13 percent in 1966, and an increase in troop numbers from 50,000 men in

1958 to 80,000 in 1966 (ibid.: 245). The wars with Israel in 1967 and 1973, in which Iraqi contingents participated (fighting on the Syrian front), increased defense spending to 19 percent of GDP and troop strength to 200,000 men. Between 1974 and 1980, defense spending fell, but the army continued to grow. With the outbreak of the Iran-Iraq War in September 1980, defense expenditure rose again sharply. By 1980 the government had raised military spending more than sixfold over the 1975 level to US$19.8 billion, or nearly 39 percent of GDP (Al-nasrawi 2001: 206). The proportion of military spending of GDP continued to rise; by the 1980s such spending absorbed between one-half and two-thirds of GDP. In addition, political rule was based on personal relationships with trusted individuals and remained aloof from formal institutions. Despite the existence of such institutions, a key role was played by informal relationships, networks of patronage, and social and geographical origins. In 1987, for example, one-third of RCC and Ba'th regional command members came from Tikrit, the home town of Saddam Hussein (Yapp 1991: 243). These appointees shared not only geographical origin, but also allegiance to the same Al-Bu Nasir tribe. The brutality and the growing capacity of the Iraqi state under the rule of Saddam Hussein (1978–2003) have been amply documented (Al-Khalil 1989). Fear and violence became the regime's source of authority; from the highest state officials to all quarters of society, a culture of terror emerged. This state-making project was based on extreme forms of violence and used an aggressive foreign policy as a way of channeling domestic discontent and accruing additional resources through external rent-seeking. While resembling European state making to some degree, this process did not produce embedded authority structures or what Tilly has termed the "civilianization of government and domestic politics" (Tilly 1990: 206).

Iraq as a Failed State

Much of Iraq's modern history (1958–80) has followed the rentier state paradigm. The early years of independent Iraq were characterized by a reliance on domestic resource extraction, but the discovery of oil in 1927, the subsequent development of Iraq's oil industry, and the nationalization of that industry in 1961 set Iraq on the path of the rentier state. Rulers used the abundance of oil revenues to develop distributive capacities and allowed for political rule to become personalized and based on patronage networks. But as the Iraqi rentier state entered fiscal difficulties, the regime turned toward war making as a state-making strategy. War making was first employed internally, then soon externally. However, while this strategy might have been feasible in early modern Europe (Tilly 1975; McNeill 1983; Ertman 1997), such was no longer the case in the twentieth century. The Iran-Iraq War (1980–88) considerably weakened Iraq's state capacity and thereby had the inverse effect of wars conducted in early modern Europe (Al-Khafaji 2000; Gongora 1997; Owen 2000). The international system within which Iraq was operating was much different and less conducive to a strategy of war making than Europe; territorial borders were given and guaranteed by external powers (L. C. Brown 1984; Lustick 1997). Hence, Iraq's war making in 1990–91 brought about a response from the international community and contributed to the demise of the rentier state ten years later. State failure in Iraq came about through an internal process in which the state lost its ability to function properly, but the collapse of state institutions came at the hands of external powers.[3]

*   *   *

In order to grasp the declining welfare function of the Iraqi state that led to its failure, it is necessary to provide a brief description of the Iraqi provinces of the Ottoman Empire. The three Ottoman provinces that were to make up Iraq were endowed with favorable climatic conditions and cultivable soil. The basic conditions for economic development, based on a mixture of favorable geographical location and a comparative advantage in agricultural production, were in place. Between 1864 and 1913 Ottoman Iraq had a mixed trade balance, but from 1913 to 1939 the territory had a negative trade balance (Hasan 1958: 355; El-Haj 1961).

Prior to the discovery of oil and the start of exploration in 1927, Iraq made use of its comparative advantage in agriculture, which it gradually lost thereafter. Income taxes were first introduced in 1909, under Ottoman rule. After World War I these were abolished; an income law was only reinstated in 1927. Modifications and refinements came in 1939 and 1943; an intermediate law was passed in 1956 and eventually a regular tax law in 1968. Until the 1960s income taxes made a modest contribution to the ordinary budget; they ranged from 3.4 to 5 percent depending on the year (Sharif 1968: 543, 549).

While the early years of independent Iraq were characterized by a reliance on domestic resource extraction, the discovery of oil in 1927, and the subsequent development of an oil industry and its nationalization in 1961, put Iraq on the track of a rentier state.[4] The fiscal nature of the state changed during the 1950s, with oil royalties no longer being treated as extra-budgetary receipts but now incorporated into the budgetary process. This gave the state considerable financial resources that it ploughed into social welfare, through a newly created state agency (the Iraqi Development Board), which was given the task of coordinating spending (Qubain 1958). The change in the fiscal nature of the state brought the first signs of the creation of a rentier state: a spending spree and a decline in the non-oil sector. Oil revenues prior to 1962 were modest; they increased to about 60 percent of total revenues during the 1960s and 1970s, while domestic revenue extraction continued modestly (Askari, Cummings, and Glover 1982: 108). From 1973 onwards, however, Iraq's fiscal system showed clear signs of rentierism, with oil revenues ranging from 56 percent in 1972–73 to almost 86 percent in 1977 and taxes falling considerably in percentage relative to total revenues. Taxes were still levied on personal incomes and profits of companies and, in theory, rates were steeply progressive. In reality, taxes were collected only from salaried employees of the state.[5] The reach of the state was short and extended only as far as its own salaried personnel. Agricultural incomes, except for land rentals, were excluded from taxation and in the private sector taxes were levied only inconsistently and inefficiently. In essence, personal income tax became the burden of a portion of the middle class working in the state administration (Batatu 1978: 105–8).[6]

Iraq profited not only from the increase in oil revenues from the mid-1970s onwards, but also from earnings generated by assets held overseas. Initially, these earnings remained minor in relation to total revenues (4 percent in 1976), but sharply increased following the

Table 2.1. Oil revenues in Iraq, 1950–77 (as percentage of total revenues)

1950	1962	1970	1973	1977	Average
17.3	64.1	53.7	80.9	85.5	60.3

Source: Waterbury 1997: 155.

second oil crisis in 1979 (the current-account surplus stood at 3,360 million dinars in 1979 and at 4,370 million dinars in 1980). At the beginning of the 1980s, Iraqi foreign holdings had increased to a level where they represented 45 percent of oil revenues and 39 percent of total government revenue (Askari, Cummings, and Glover 1982: 111). Figures for oil revenues are summarized in table 2.1.

This drastic increase in additional resources allowed the Iraqi state to embark on a state-making project based on large-scale spending, implemented in a top-down fashion and largely divorced from societal demands. The massive influx of oil revenues during the 1970s enabled Iraq to pursue a policy of "guns and butter"—extravagant spending on expanding its military-security apparatus and on welfare benefits (social development).[7] Internally, expanded military-security expenditure was designed to strengthen the power of the ruling Ba'thist regime. On the external front, greater expenditure was used to engage in aggressive foreign policies, which led to the outbreak of war with Iran in 1980.

Given the massive flow of oil revenues, it seemed it would be easy to bear the costs of a war with Iran. Surplus funds also came in the form of strategic rents (foreign military aid) from neighboring states. During the first two years of the war, Iraq's economic position was comfortable. It used its oil exports and an annual oil income of US$30 billion to finance the war effort (Al-Khafaji 2000: 273). However, as the war dragged on, Iraq's economic position began to deteriorate as a result of war damage to its oil-export facilities and a decline in world oil prices in 1985. Additionally, Syria (allied with Iran) closed the pipeline to the Mediterranean Sea, thereby reducing Iraq's export capabilities to less than 30 percent of production capacity. The total costs of the war, which lasted from 1980 to 1988, were estimated at US$452.6 billion for Iraq and US$644.3 billion for Iran; this includes the cost of damage to both countries' infrastructure and losses to GDP (Mofid 1990). These figures exceed the total amount of oil revenue both countries accrued since they started selling their oil by a total of US$678.5 billion (Sluglett and Farouk-Sluglett 1990: 20).

By the end of the war Iraq was faced with economic difficulties, not least the problem of demobilizing about 200,000 soldiers (Chaudhry 1990: 155). The state was not able to accommodate so large a number of soldiers, who all depended on government-guaranteed jobs and welfare benefits. The state could no longer deliver on the social contract it had established during the boom years of the rentier economy. War had fundamentally altered the situation and redefined normality. Unemployment, the effects of which had already been felt during the war due to privatization measures enacted in 1986–87, but aggravated thereafter, became widespread in Iraq and young people were deprived of previously guaranteed careers in the civil service. It seemed the only possible strategy was to keep young Iraqis in the service of the state—albeit not in a civilian function, but in the armed services. The Iran-Iraq War undoubtedly eroded the fiscal basis of the state. Probably a few years of peace and normal oil production would have brought the fiscal situation back to pre-war levels, but instead of using an inward-looking strategy of coping with the fiscal crisis brought about by the Iran-Iraq War, the regime chose an extravert and belligerent strategy of rent acquisition by invading Kuwait in August 1990.

*　*　*

The history of Iraq between 1980 and 2003 demonstrates how a chain of reactions caused the failure of the rentier state: initial war making (the Iran-Iraq War) led to an overstretch of state capacity, and the ensuing fiscal crisis led to a further weakening of the state and pushed the regime into bellicosity—the annexation of oil-rich Kuwait to shore up Iraq's rentier resources. The concerted military action by the international community and the subsequent UN sanctions regime left the Iraqi state crippled. Having lost the First Gulf War to the U.S.-led United Nations multinational force, the regime of Saddam Hussein was hamstrung by multiple international sanctions, and could exercise only limited state functions. The weakened Iraqi state had to re-create new forms of legitimacy by resorting to Iraqi nationalism based on tribal affinities and Islam, to counter the persistent surveillance by and encroachment of the powerful external enemies led by the United States.

The decision to invade Kuwait in 1990 had its origins in the fiscal crisis of the Iraqi state. Quite typically for a rentier state, concerns about the relative decline in oil revenues available for political allocation and the large number of soldiers who needed employment in the civilian sector were crucial in the perceived decline of regime security. While Iraq had initially attempted to counter the fiscal crisis of the mid-1980s with traditional, internal-oriented measures (extended economic reform and privatization efforts since 1987), it had to turn outwards in order to avoid societal implosion (Chaudhry 1990: 151–55). The perceived decline in regime security is highlighted in the following statement by the then deputy prime minister, Taha Ramadan:

> How were we going to maintain the loyalty of the people and their support for the leader if they saw the inability of the leadership to provide a minimal standard of living in this rich country? (Gause 2002: 59)

Welfare considerations, the allocation of resources, and regime security are clearly linked here. Allocation of resources and stability are key features of rentier states; resource allocation contributes to such states' stability as long as abundant resources are available. When resources decline, the link turns backwards toward domestic insecurities. The fact that Iraq's small leadership group felt threatened by declining powers to allocate resources and felt it had to turn outwards to acquire more resources is highlighted in Ramadan's statement.

Following the invasion of Kuwait, coercion came to be felt in another way. With the temporary destabilization of Iraq in the aftermath of the international invasion in 1991, the country's two largest ethnocultural groups, the Kurds in the north and the Shi'ites in the south, rose up against the regime of Saddam Hussein. Despite assurances of international support, they were eventually left on their own to be violently crushed by Iraq's Republican Guards. Repression and coercion became institutionalized in Iraq again during the 1990s, as the regime targeted any form of opposition and committed numerous human rights abuses (Human Rights Watch 2003, 2004).

*   *   *

Coercion came to be felt in yet another, collective way after the end of the invasion of Kuwait. The international efforts to counter the invasion had two goals: concerted military action, led by the United States, to expel Iraq from Kuwait, and the imposition of a UN sanctions regime to control the ceasefire agreement. It is the latter sanctions regime that had the most profound influence on the unmaking of the Iraqi state during the 1990s.

On 6 August 1990 the UN Security Council adopted Resolution 661, which imposed mandatory sanctions on Iraq under Chapter VII of the UN Charter and established a Sanctions Committee to monitor implementation of the resolution. More than 300 items were included on a list of banned goods compiled by the committee, the strategic rationale being the prohibition on material that could be used for military purposes. The initial resolution, UNSCR 666 (1990), was amended on 13 September to allow for foodstuffs to be supplied to members of the civilian population of Iraq under the age of 15, in order "to relieve human suffering." A UN mission visited Iraq on 10–17 March 1991 and reported that "the Iraqi people may soon face a further imminent catastrophe, which could include epidemic and famine, if massive life-supporting needs are not rapidly met." Consequently, the Security Council decided to exempt foodstuffs and medical supplies from the sanctions regime (Resolution 687), and four years later, with Resolution 986 (1995), established the "oil-for-food" program.[8]

The impact of the sanctions regime was profound, particularly on the Iraqi economy and the state's ability to provide welfare to its citizens. This extended into all spheres of social, economic, and civilian life in Iraq: employment reached an estimated 70 percent (Hoskins 1997), Iraq's GNP fell from US$435 billion in 1989 to US$17 billion in 1993, water-treatment capability collapsed so that an estimated 2.5 million Iraqis had no access to potable water,[9] the availability of food declined, and economic life was reduced to basically two sectors: the oil sector (through the oil-for-food program after 1995) and the agricultural sector (through subsistence economy and small-scale trade). Estimates of the number of deaths due to the sanctions regime are as high as 1.5 million people, including more than 500,000 children. The World

Health Organization (WHO) concluded that the health system was set back by some 50 years (Alnasrawi 2001: 214). Indeed, the Iraqi state's infrastructure as well as its economic capacity—figures indicate that per-capita GDP in the 1990s was lower than that of 1950—were so curtailed that half a century's work in state building and centralization of modern state institutions seems to have been unmade within a decade. While it is clear that the dire economic situation of much of the Iraqi population had its origins in the mid-1980s (an indication of this being the attempts at economic reform in 1986–87), the real magnitude of the decline in state infrastructure became evident under the sanctions regime, at which time the Iraqi state was limited in fulfilling the most basic welfare needs of its citizens.

The unmaking of the Iraqi state had to do with declining state capacity to fulfill core functions, and is better described as a functional failure of the state. The collapse of the Iraqi state, in institutional terms, occurred with the U.S.-led invasion in March 2003 and the dismantling of state institutions in May 2003. Particularly important in this context was the inability of the United States to maintain the welfare-allocation mechanism, which, while weak and limited, had still functioned at quasi-state level during the 1990s.[10]

External Intervention and the Reconstruction of the State

Iraq's history after the fall of Saddam Hussein's regime in 2003 has seen many of the features of earlier state making: a distributive welfare state actively trying to define and build a nation in a top-down fashion, a society which is highly mobilized and atomized, and sectarian problems and tensions characterizing both state and society. In addition, there are major challenges facing reconstruction: Kurdish-Arab tensions; disputed internal borders; corruption; institutional development; friction between federal, regional, and local administrations; and challenges from neighbors. The greatest difference between pre- and post-Saddam Iraq has been in the realm of security: the fall of the regime has brought about a security vacuum which neither the U.S.-led forces nor the renascent Iraqi military have so far been able to fill.[11]

The security function of the state has largely remained unfulfilled, with insecurity rampant and kidnappings and arbitrary killings occurring daily. Security is a precondition for the state fulfilling its other two functions (welfare and representation), as detailed in chapter 1. Consequently, state reconstruction in post-Saddam Iraq has proven to be particularly difficult and its current trajectory remains undetermined. Senior U.S. officials have indeed questioned whether Iraq will ever be free of violence, as violence was also characteristic of the regime of Saddam Hussein,[12] and have acknowledged the difficult path to reconstruction of a stable state.[13] Instability and terrorism remain largely foreign-grown, according to research by Associated Press on the insurgencies in Iraq in the summer of 2005. It is estimated that insurgents number around 1,000 persons, whereas Iraqi fighters make up the much larger figure of some 10,000. Interestingly, only about 10 percent of suicide attacks are committed by Iraqis. There are about 20 noteworthy groups of insurgents but with minimal foreign components. Indeed, the core of the insurgency is a "successful fusion of nationalist and religious sentiment among Sunni Arabs" (Hashim 2006). Coalition officials in Iraq estimated that by mid-2004 the core group numbered 12,000 to 16,000, possibly even 20,000 (Posch 2005: 37). Three separate sources of violence exist: organized crime and industrial-scale criminal gangs, which operate in the urban centers of Basra, Baghdad, and Mosul and make a living through kidnapping and other forms of racketeering; remnants of the Ba'th regime, which have been reconstituted through "personal, family and geographic ties"; and Islamist forces (Dodge 2004; Posch 2005: 25–41). All three sources arguably originate in the unmaking of the state as it was under Saddam Hussein: the organized criminal groups arose in the mid-1990s, during the sanctions decade, when Saddam Hussein's grip on society was at its weakest; the personal ties that unite former Ba'th supporters are a result of the party's penetration into all aspects of society and of the simultaneous influence of networks of patronage and personalized ties; and, finally, the re-Islamization of society and the politicization of religious life during the 1990s laid the groundwork for Islamist-inspired insurgencies in the aftermath of 2003. The vast number of insurgents makes it difficult to speak of a unified front; there is also great variation in group size and in ideology between and within insurgent groups (Posch 2005: 107–13). The sole unifying element is the desire for foreign forces to leave the country and for the country to be rendered ungovernable (Hashim 2006). Recruitment for the insurgents is aided by the informal nature of Iraqi society, which is based on family, personal ties, and informal relations (Finlan 2005). Another key feature of the insecurity in post-2003 Iraq is that it is difficult to draw boundaries between armed tribesmen, criminal gangs, Islamist insurgents, and nationalist groups (Posch 2005: 43). Despite expectations of stability and order, 2004's formal handover of sovereignty to an interim Iraqi government did little to change the situation of insecurity. Car-bombings, terrorist attacks, kidnappings, and killings remain part of the insecurities that plagued the country. In 2006, the bombing of the Golden Mosque in Samarra triggered an escalating wave of sectarian violence; many observers have judged the situation to be one of low-intensity civil war.[14] The former UK ambassador to Iraq, William Patey, wrote in a confidential communication that the "prospects for a low intensity civil war and a de facto division of Iraq is probably more likely at this stage than a successful and substantial transition to a stable democracy."[15] The U.S. military commander at the time, Gen. John Abizaid, judged that due to the rise of sectarian violence it was possible that Iraq had moved toward civil war.[16] And Iraqi officials saw the violence as purely based on "killings according to identity cards."[17] Since 2007, the security situation has slightly improved due to the strategy of incorporating important Sunni tribes into the Shi'ite-dominated ruling regime (the so-called "Sunni Awakening"). This awakening started in the Sunni-dominated province of Al-Anbar, but gradually extended to Baghdad. It has been credited with reducing the overall level of sectarian violence and of changing a low-intensity civil war into a classic insurgency. The Iraqi security forces are slowly increasing their capacity to pacify and control the whole country. Some progress has been achieved but it remains fragile and reversible. At the time of writing, half of the country's police force is in the process of being formed and cannot yet be deployed. The other half, plus two-thirds of the armed forces, are able to fight the insurgency only with the help of the United States. Currently, the number of Iraqi policemen and soldiers stands at 171,500; this was expected to rise to 270,000 by 2011.[18] The prospects for ending the insurgency and for reinstating security completely remain slim. Observers therefore expect low levels of violence to remain characteristic of Iraq even in the long term and as state reconstruction proceeds.

*　　*　　*

In economic terms, post-2003 Iraq has seen challenges and problems similar to those the country faced throughout the 1970s and 1980s. Among these are irregularities in the budget, an economy almost exclusively reliant on oil production and export, and rising unemployment. The Coalition Provisional Authority (CPA), which ruled Iraq from April 2003 to June 2004, came under fire when some US$8.8 billion designated for the ministry's budget could not be accounted for. In early July 2005 the Iraqi state saw mounting confusion at the Ministry of Oil over the prospective auction of 11 of the state's southern oilfields. An initial report by Reuters that an international bidding round would soon be held to grant concessions to international oil companies was contradicted by subsequent reports citing officials who claimed that no such round would take place. The initial report, on 13 June, quoted the ministry's director of oilfield development, Hazim Sultan, as saying Baghdad would open the 11 oilfields to international participation. However, a subsequent report on 10 July denied the auction, citing ʿAbdullah al-ʿAmir, foreign relations adviser to Oil Minister Ibrahim Bahr al-ʿUlum. These measures, crucial for the attraction of foreign investors, were clear signs of ministerial infighting and unclear competence structures within the state bureaucracy. The auction planned in 2005 was eventually called off; the incident highlighted the confusion in Baghdad as the state tried to increase oil production. In 2009, when the auction was finally held, it was conducted calmly and without the bureaucratic confusion that had reigned in 2005; in all, 44 companies took part in the bidding in 2009, and Royal Dutch Shell and Malaysia's Petronas won the right to develop one of the world's largest remaining untapped oilfields (Majnoon in southern Iraq), which promises to increase oil output considerably over the next decades.

Another example of the bureaucratic confusion which reigned in Iraq in the attempt to reconstruct functioning state institutions was the CPA's Program Review Board—a 12-member panel of U.S. and other Allied officials charged with dispensing money for reconstruction efforts. The board's minutes show that the Program Review Board increased its spending in the final few days of its existence and that there were few objections to the spending. In the final meeting of the board, the United Kingdom's and Australia's advisers managed to shut down two CPA-backed projects: a US$10 million plan to create a museum documenting atrocities committed by the former regime, and a US$41 million dump that may have been intended to dispose of hazardous waste generated by the military coalition (Cooper and Jaffe 2004).

Despite signs of economic recovery, electricity cuts, food shortages, and unemployment remain problems. Oil production has not fully recovered. It stood at 2.3 million barrels a day (bb/d) in February 2004, but has since declined (Economist Intelligence Unit 2004a: 33). High expectations of a rise in Iraq's oil production to 2.5 million bb/d and beyond have only gradually been met: production stood at 1.5 million bb/d in December 2005, 1.8 million bb/d in March 2006, 2.0 million bb/d in March 2007, 2.4 million bb/d in March 2008, and 2.5 million bb/d since mid-2009.[19] Oil revenues now account for almost 95 percent of all government revenues and 60 percent of GDP, but the oil sector employs only 1 percent of the Iraqi workforce. Iraq has reverted to a rentier state in which jobs in the public sector are seen as patronage and welfare opportunities, and where oil rents are distributed according to political criteria or in some cases are mishandled due to corruption. Consequently, some observers have already predicted that Iraq will once again fall victim to the oil curse.[20] The slow growth and weakness of the economy have affected welfare in Iraq. The post-2003 situation resembles the sanctions decade in the 1990s, with ever more children suffering from malnutrition. The United Nations has estimated that the number of children under the age of five suffering from malnutrition doubled within two years following the U.S.-led invasion (United Nations 2005). Creating a stable security situation is certainly a prerequisite for economic progress. Working toward this goal requires either maintaining the old allocation rentier order or developing agriculture and industry as new sources of employment, income, and export goods.

*   *   *

Progress has been achieved in terms of representation, and the new Iraqi state seems on a path of gradual democratization. However, the creation of a democratic process has proven difficult, with a few optimistic signs: the handover of sovereignty in June 2004, national elections in January 2005 with the establishment of a transitional government, the ratification of a constitution in the summer of 2005, national elections in December 2005, and the re-establishment of the government of Iraq in May 2006. Nonetheless, the process of state making since 2003 has been overshadowed by the issue of security and the establishment of a monopoly on the legitimate use of force. Questions about the future of U.S. and other Allied troops in Iraq have become more urgent than ever. Since the presence of foreign troops is clearly a de-legitimizing factor for the new Iraqi government, a reduction in U.S. and other Allied troop numbers, coupled with a feasible timeframe for withdrawal, might be the best available solution. However, in view of the security situation on the ground, an immediate pullout does not seem to be the answer. A clear signal to the Iraqi government and people that the stationing of foreign troops in Iraq is time-limited could boost state-making attempts on the ground, but could also create further insecurities—as suggested by developments during 2010. Indeed, the national elections of March 2010 were generally democratic but still filled with allegations of fraud, with recounts ordered and results upheld. The elections ended in a deadlock between incumbent Prime Minister Nouri al-Maliki and candidate Ayad 'Allawi. Additionally, forming a government took nine months and proved difficult as fundamental questions remained about the outcome of the election and the sectarian composition of the new government. Some observers have claimed that the difficulty in forming a government was linked to the heritage of fear dating from the Saddam era, during which time almost the entire new elite of post-2003 Iraq—Prime Minister al-Maliki, former interim prime minister 'Allawi, Kurdish leader Massoud Bar-zani, President Jalal Talabani, and vice-presidents Tariq al-Hashimi and 'Adil 'Abd al-Mahdi—were all victims of repression and therefore grew wary of political accommodation and compromise.

The difficulty of creating representative and legitimate state institutions became most evident during the summer of 2005. In July of that year, 12 Sunni members of the Constitution Assembly quit in order to protest at the murder of one of their colleagues, Mijbil Issa. They boycotted the Constitution Assembly until an international investigation of Issa's murder was set up. The importance of a Sunni presence in the reconstruction efforts was obvious, since Sunnis represent 20 percent of the population; in two of Iraq's 18 provinces (Salahuddin and Al-Anbar), Sunnis are the majority. There was eventual agreement on the final text of the constitution, but the process was marred by incertitude and other obstacles. When the text was finally adopted by the drafting committee at the end of August 2005, only three of the 15 Sunni members of the drafting committee attended the signing ceremony and none of them signed it. On 28 August 2005 the text was read to the National Assembly, with a view to its submission to a popular referendum in October. The referendum eventually approved the constitution by a slight margin (three provinces rejected the text—Salahuddin and Al-Anbar provinces by two-thirds, and Nineveh province by 55 percent—thereby barely missing the two-thirds necessary to block the adoption of the constitution). However, it became evident that many of the key problems, despite having been put in writing, were still present. The tight schedule for the elaboration of a constitution (less than a full year) and the short period of consultation bore heavily.

* * *

The key remaining issues in contention and the two major challenges to state making in contemporary Iraq are federalism and the role of Islam in society. With regard to federalism, the first questions that arose related to the regional elections of January 2005. Besides the general parliamentary elections for the National Assembly, regional elections were held for the Kurdish parliament and communal elections for the city council in Kirkuk. It was the latter two elections which brought past grievances to the surface. As a result of the Arabization campaign of the 1970s, which involved deportation of Kurds to the south and the redrawing of the boundaries of Iraq's provinces, many Kurds were no longer formally registered in Kirkuk or the surrounding al-Ta'mim province (prior to the Arabization campaign the province had simply been called "Kirkuk province") and were therefore not eligible to vote in the two elections (Van Bruinessen 2005: 55). They formally protested to the Iraqi Electoral Commission and only after 2000, when persons were added to the election list in al-Ta'mim province, was the problem resolved. As the Kurdish parties had used election day for a referendum on Kurdish independence (95 percent voted in favor of this), the federalist position came to be undermined from another angle. Indeed, formal petitions for Kurdish independence were handed over to the United Nations in December 2004 (New York) and January 2005 (Geneva), but still did not lead to the formation of an independent Kurdish state.[21] The referendum on Kurdish independence—although not formally recognized—increased international visibility for the Kurdish case and underlined to many policymakers the importance of maintaining the Kurdish minority within a unified Iraq.

The second question related to federalism, in view of the fact that Kurdish autonomy within the borders of Iraq seems the only realistic option for the time being, is the exact demarcation of such an autonomous area. During consultations on the permanent constitution of Iraq, Kurdish representatives introduced a map which they wanted used as part of the basis of that document. This map showed the Kurdish region extending beyond its current area of demarcation and including the cities of Badra and Jassan (150 kilometers south of Baghdad). Fears have been expressed over a strong application of federalism, as it is seen to weaken the central Iraqi state and particularly the state's ability to accrue resources. Although the constitution generally anticipated that oil revenues would accrue to the federal government, it also assigned a considerable role to the regions.[22] The issue was therefore one of effective control, representation, and access to wealth and resources. Indeed, the Kurdish Regional Government (KRG) has laid claim to the oil and gas underlying its own territories and the KRG has already signed several oil contracts with foreign states and with companies from the

United States and the People's Republic of China. While some observers dispute the legality of these contracts, the deals remain as testimony
to state-making activities and highlight the interplay between rule and
revenue; beyond this the interplay between welfare and representation,
so common in rentier state making, is also obvious in post-2003 Iraq.

The conflict over the role of Islam in the new state institutions is essentially pursued by the Shi'ite population. This group had long been
treated as a minority within Iraq (despite actually being in the majority, as indicated already by the earliest censuses of 1920 and 1931), and
had at times been repressed. Since 2003 the Shi'ites have affirmed their
demands more vehemently. The political conflict between Shi'ites and
Sunnis in Iraq during the 1960s, 1970s and 1980s turned into a genuinely religious conflict in the aftermath of the U.S.-led invasion of 2003.
Today Muslim clerics play a crucial role in Iraqi politics, as indicated
by the profiles of figures such as Ayatollah Sayyid Ali al-Husayni al-
Sistani, 'Abdel-Aziz al-Hakim, or Muqtadar al-Sadr. Sistani especially
has played a crucial role in state-building attempts in the post-2003
era. Not only did he give his approval to the handover of sovereignty
to the Iraqi Interim Government in June 2004, but he has also influenced policies on national elections and the drafting of the constitution. Interestingly, however, Sistani subscribes to a view that sees clerics
as not engaged in the political realm—in contrast to the situation in
the Islamic Republic of Iran—and has imposed limitations on himself
and other clerics, to prevent clerics becoming too closely entangled
in everyday politics. Instead of Khomeini's rule by clerics (*wilayat al-
faqih*), Sistani propagates the rule of clerics in social affairs (*wilayat
al-faqih fi al-masa'il al-ijtima'iyya*). Indeed, Sistani's office in the city
of Najaf serves as an informal government agency, controlling an array
of hospitals, student dormitories, libraries, research centers, schools,
and refugee centers in Iran and Iraq (Buchta 2004: 343–55). Ayatollah
Sistani was born in 1930 in Mashhad, Iran, into a family of clerics that
traces its ancestry back to the prophet Muhammad. Sistani was educated at Mashhad and Qum in Iran and in Najaf, Iraq, under Grand
Ayatollah Abu al-Qasim al-Kho'i. On the death of al-Kho'i in 1992,
Sistani became his teacher's successor. In the aftermath of the 2003 regime change, Sistani became an influential figure in the reconstruction

of Iraq: by negotiating a ceasefire between U.S. forces and the Sadr militias in Najaf, by issuing fatwas in favor of participating in the elections, and by calling on Shiʿites to show restraint after several attacks against Shiʿites and Shiʿite shrines. International and domestic observers agree that state reconstruction needs to involve a measure of just government or constitutional rule. What exactly this would look like is less clear, although it did seem clear from the outset that the future of the Iraqi state would not be a secular one.

*   *   *

The success of building legitimate and representative institutions in Iraq will ultimately depend on how the country's three largest ethnic groups—Arab Sunnis, Arab Shiʿites, and Kurds—will accommodate their various demands. The questions of federalism and of the role of religion in the state are central here. Finally, the reconciliation process of finding justice for past injustices and repression, as symbolized by the Iraqi Special Tribunal, is equally important but difficult at the same time, as it has the potential for alienating the country's Sunni population. Political inclusiveness, both in terms of representation and justice, is therefore the highest priority. Signs of progress along this road could mean greater Sunni political inclusiveness through a redrafted constitution or the re-deployment of coalition troops within Iraq, accompanied by a transfer to Iraqi military control in certain provinces, and the removal of some coalition troops from the country altogether. U.S. President Barack Obama's announcement that U.S. military forces would be withdrawn by the end of 2011 has certainly paved the way for the latter, as has the 2008 Strategic Framework Agreement between the United States and Iraq, which foresees a long-term relationship in training and support but a largely reduced operational presence of coalition forces in Iraq.

It is clear in the modern history of state making in Iraq that rentierism and war making have weakened the state, leading to its failure and ultimately its collapse in 2003. In contrast to the European experience in the early modern period, war did not serve to pacify and unify the country. The reasons for this can be found in three factors: the creation of the British mandate in 1920, the establishment of Iraq's institutions against the will of several ethnocultural minorities living in the country, and the creation of an unrepresentative system under Ba'thist rule. The history of Ba'thist Iraq confirms certain insights gained from modern European state making—namely, how war-makers were supplanted by state-makers. Under the leadership of Saddam Hussein, the Ba'th party managed to curb the influence of professional soldiers in politics and to civilianize the country's leadership. The centralization of the state reached its peak under the Ba'thist regime, following the party's gaining of power in 1968. However, the aggressive foreign policy pursued by the Ba'thist regime also contributed to its demise. Iraq's path of state making—war and the breakdown of the rentier state—started in 1980s with the outward extension of violence and the engagement in a war with Iran. The eventual demise of the Ba'thist regime can be attributed to organized violence, starting with the Iran-Iraq War (1980–88) and leading to the invasion of Kuwait (1990); to the subsequent sanctions regime; and eventually to the U.S.-led invasion of Iraq in 2003. War making in the Iraqi case and the *raison d'état* have thereby become thoroughly and disastrously integrated in ways that differ both qualitatively and quantitatively from any other Middle Eastern state. In addition, war making and the projection of organized violence outside of Iraq's borders have been augmented in unique ways by internal violence as a form of governance. Under Saddam Hussein state making was for decades decoupled from the demands of society and aimed at a transformation of that society. With declining oil revenues in the late 1980s, and especially during the decade of sanctions in the 1990s, the Iraqi state was seriously restricted in its ability to fulfill its most basic functions (ensuring welfare, security, and representation). Nevertheless, Iraq had managed to maintain a minimal level of statehood and order. Only after the U.S.-led invasion of March 2003, followed by the CPA's dismantling of Iraqi state institutions in May 2003, did Iraq become a collapsed state, in which the situation resembled that of a war of all against all.

This chapter has ultimately shown that in cases where weak rentier states employ war making as a strategy for state making, this has effects opposite to those of the ruler-subject struggles characteristic of early modern Europe: where rentierism is coupled with war making, the outcome for state building is hypertrophied militarism and large-scale repression. However, this militarism is not sustainable: it breaks down allocation channels and reduces general welfare levels, as oil revenues are spent on Scuds and not on butter (Sadowski 1993). Thus, rentierism leads not only to institutionally weak states, but in some cases to state failure and the breakdown of the rentier state.

3

Jordan

Rentierism and State Survival

Let's face it: works on Jordan have rarely gained the kind of recognition among Middle East scholars as those about Egypt, Palestine and Syria, to name just a few countries [. . .] Jordan serves as an excellent case study for discussions about state construction, the development of nationalism and national identity.

Betty Anderson, "The evolution of Jordanian studies"

Jordan, like Iraq, has been engaged in war making since its independence. It was involved in the 1948 War with Israel, the 1967 Six-Day War (June War) with Israel, the military campaign against the PLO and Syria in September 1970, and the 1973 Yom Kippur War with Israel.[1] From the "war-makes-states" perspective one would again expect the emergence of a strong state. However, here the opposite is the case: Jordan shows clear elements of institutional state weakness in the domains of representation and welfare, similarly to Iraq prior to the invasion of Kuwait in 1990. While Jordan has managed to avoid state failure as in the case of Iraq, it is still characterized by weak statehood.

*   *   *

This chapter focuses on how Jordan has managed its survival as a state. The chapter proceeds as follows: the first part places Jordan in its regional context. The chapter shows that the actual level of rentierism (including political rents, transnational financial flows, and worker remittances) is higher than in other states of the Middle East. The chapter goes on to argue that these additional rents available to state-builders allowed Jordan to maintain a degree of militarization and administrative statehood, which—in the absence of historical precursors to modern statehood—assured the country's survival as an independent state. This was achieved by incorporating key social groups into the state bureaucracy through welfare entitlements and allocations. The final part of this chapter considers how Jordan has coped with the decline in state resources (and hence in welfare spending) over the previous decade and how the state has attempted to forge a national identity in order to compensate for this.

War and State Making in Jordan

The Emirate of Transjordan (later the Kingdom of Jordan) was created in 1921 along with boundaries and state institutions. For the British and the Hashemite rulers, the creation of Transjordan as a state involved the simultaneous creation of a nation. In the case of most other states, state creation is preceded by a nationalist movement or requires a pre-existing sense of national identity; however, in the case of Jordan no such things existed. There was no country or other territory called "Transjordan" or ethnic group referred to as "Transjordanians" (Massad 2001: 27–28); prior to 1921 only "rudimentary and fragmented governmental structures" existed in what was to become Jordan. Modern state institutions and a nation had to be built up from scratch. The pillars of the new state were the British advisors—"the King's men" (Satloff 1994)—who protected the Hashemite regime until well into the 1950s. Tribal elements in Jordan also contributed to stability on the path to state making (Peake 1958; Tell 2000; Vatikiotis 1967). Political control over the tribes was achieved in Jordan via a mixture of coercion and conciliation. The pacification of the tribes was particularly conducive to state-formation in the early years in that it helped in controlling the borders of the new state and maintained the domestic monopoly on violence within the country. In subsequent years the political support of the tribes contributed in large degree to the survival of the Jordanian state (Susser 2000).

*   *   *

Almost as important as the British advisors were the Jordanian Army—which created loyalty toward the state on the part of the tribal leaders—and a ruler who became the "centrifugal force radiating" from Amman by distributing services and financial benefits (Anderson 2002: 241).

Historically, the British were the state-builders in Transjordan. In 1920 they established a small mobile force of former Ottoman soldiers and local townspeople under the leadership of a British officer, Frederick Peake. This force was the precursor of the Arab Legion (al-Jaysh al-'Arabi), which was formally created in 1921 and later became the national army of Jordan (Vatikiotis 1967). The Arab Legion was initially designed as a police force to keep order among the Transjordanian tribes, to suppress Bedouin raiding, and to police the borders of the new state (Axelrod 1978). The Arab Legion was an attempt at imposing the monopoly on the legitimate use of violence within the territory of Transjordan. As with the history of state making in the Gulf, conceptions of territorial boundaries and sovereignty were largely alien to Transjordan's tribal society. Territorial control proved difficult during the first decade and was challenged on numerous occasions, particularly through Wahhabi raids in the south (Layne 1994).

The Arab Legion was transformed into a regular army under the leadership of another British officer, John Bagot Glubb (Glubb 1948). Glubb, who had previous experience with Bedouin tribes in Iraq, was called in to run the Desert Patrol Force in 1930 and the Arab Legion in 1939. He changed the recruitment method to draw largely on Bedouins; eventually 30–40 percent of soldiers came from a Bedouin background, making such soldiers the backbone of the new army. After he took control in 1939 the Arab Legion expanded fivefold, to 8,000 men, with 3,000 in the Bedouin mechanized brigade (Tell 2000: 237). During World War II the Arab Legion fought in Iraq and Syria and came to be known as the best-trained Arab army. Following the creation of the Kingdom of Jordan in 1946, by the renaming of the Emirate of Transjordan, the Arab Legion was transformed into the regular army of the newly independent state. It fought in the 1948 War with Israel.

The establishment of the Arab Legion underlines the importance of militarization in the initial stages of state making. The Arab Legion was transformed from a small praetorian guard of 8,000–10,000 men in 1921 into a defense establishment of some 25,000 officers and men in 1956. The expanded version included three brigades, a division headquarters, an artillery corps, a signal corps and an engineer corps, as well as an air force. By 1953 each of the three brigades comprised three regiments; of the total of nine regiments, four were Bedouin. In March 1956 the strength of the Arab Legion was further increased to stand at one division and one armored brigade. Sixty-nine British officers served in the legion; many had been seconded from the British Army, while others were on contract. By May 1956, after the dismissal of Glubb, only 25 British officers remained in technical and advisory positions (Vatikiotis 1967: 7).

The degree of militarization in the early years of state making can be highlighted using government expenditures. Between 1950 and 1957 the single largest item in Jordan's budget was the Arab Legion. In 1951, the budget for the legion stood at £4,898,000 out of total budget expenditure of £9,763,000 and in 1957 at £12,272,000 with a total budget expenditure of £23,181,000 (ibid.: 10). The expansion of the army was accompanied by the incorporation of the Bedouins into the state structure (ibid.: 20). The professional military ethic and low level of political agitation within the Arab Legion served as stabilizing factors in Jordan (ibid.: 21). The legion maintained security in Jordan's interior and the integrity of the regime in the most perilous political period, 1954–57.

Tribal elements contributed to stability on the route to state consolidation. The pacification of the tribes and their incorporation into state structures during the mandate period stood in contrast to the Ottoman period, where central state authority was highly contested and by and large not accepted. As noted, political control over the tribes was achieved via a mixture of coercion and conciliation. From 1921 onwards the latter was achieved via employment in the Desert Patrol Force and the Arab Legion and through financial concessions and subsidies. In some years the income from employment in the Desert Patrol Force could indeed sustain several families (Bocco and Tell 1994: 122).

The establishment of the Arab Legion demonstrated the influence of the United Kingdom as the state-builder in Jordan, and the pacification of the Bedouins has been largely credited to the legion.[2] This legacy can still be felt in the Jordanian army today; it came to be known as a "heavily Bedouin army" (Day 1986: 81). In 1990 it was estimated that the majority of the armed forces were Bedouin (Layne 1994: 11). Senior officers were still selected from the principal tribal groups in the country and junior officers equally belonged to these tribes or extended families. Jordanian tribes represented and still represent the nucleus of the Jordanian army. The pacification of the tribes was particularly conducive to state making in the early years; it helped to control the borders of the new state and maintain domestic order, and established the monopoly on violence domestically. The political support of the tribes in subsequent years was conducive to political stability and contributed in large degree to the survival of the Jordanian state (Susser 2000).

*   *   *

Outside support was equally fundamental to stability in Jordan's state making. During the mandate era Transjordan was already "a rentier state in embryo" (Tell 2000: 182). The state received large sums in the form of strategic rents (see table 3.1), which created a linkage between welfare and representation. Initially this came from the United Kingdom in the form of a monthly subsidy; between 1922 and 1944, British grants-in-aid alone covered half of government expenditure and between 28 and 50 percent of government revenues (ibid.: 182 and 185). From the 1950s onwards Jordan received additional military aid from the United States. By 1970 Jordan ranked second only to Israel in terms of per-capita U.S. military aid. The resulting availability of a powerful security guarantor and the possibility of acquiring weapons provided the Jordanian state with security from abroad and with the financial means to allocate welfare benefits domestically.

In addition to these direct payments, the country profited from remittances from migrant workers. The escalation in oil prices in 1973 brought new opportunities for migrant labor in the Gulf states. By the end of the 1970s a third of the Jordanian labor force was employed outside of Jordan. Migrant workers' remittances grew steadily from 87 million Jordanian dinars (JD) in 1974 to almost JD 340 million in 1981. During this period remittances passing through official channels represented about 20 percent of GNP (Tell 2000: 298).

Table 3.1. State revenues and British grants to Transjordan, 1921–45 (£)

Fiscal year	Local revenues	British grants	Total revenues	Percentage British aid	Percentage local revenues
1921–22	178,789	180,000	358,789	50	50
1922–23	201,400	90,000	291,400	31	69
1923–24	—	150,000	—	—	—
1924–25	203,101	77,572	280,673	28	72
1925–26	174,502	103,957	278,459	37	63
1926–27	236,520	66,000	302,520	22	78
1927–28	237,073	45,000	282,073	16	84
1928–29	239,911	67,644	307,555	22	78
1929–30	239,172	76,975	316,147	24	76
1930–31	250,464	117,452	367,516	32	68
1931–32	222,902	115,343	338,046	34	66
1932–33	250,660	102,567	353,227	29	71
1933–34	261,507	119,905	381,412	31	69
1934–35	276,258	101,259	337,517	30	82
1935–36	313,847	81,783	395,630	21	79
1936–37	288,140	130,510	418,650	31	69
1937–38	358,160	110,990	459,150	24	76
1938–39	339,671	189,442	529,613	36	64
1939–40	400,144	223,897	623,011	36	64
1940–41	683,424	481,925	1,165,349	41	59
1941–42	389,735	536,364	1,226,099	43	32
1942–43	926,125	672,551	1,598,674	42	58
1943–44	1,478,783	754,194	2,232,977	34	66
1944–45	1,644,548	933,061	2,577,609	36	64
1945–46	1,794,684	1,543,861	3,338,545	46	54

Sources: Adapted from Amawi (1993: 275) and Tell (2000: 185). Note that the figures for the years 1934–35 and 1941–42 do not add up to 100 percent.

Migrant workers' remittances are of course a form of rent that does not flow directly to the state and is thus not under the state's direct control. Nevertheless, oil revenues have been recycled to many non-oil states in the Middle East via migrant workers' remittances and have thereby propagated rentier behavior across the whole of the Arab world (Beblawi 1990: 98). These remittances flow directly to society. For the worker these remittances constitute income earned for effort and labor;

for the state they are akin to aid or non-requited money transfers (ibid.: 97). Such remittances have a stabilizing effect on the national economy and are courted by the state through exemptions granted to tourism and to foreign banks. But remittances can also induce a level of instability due to their unpredictability; this is demonstrated by the example of the expulsion of Yemeni and Jordanian workers from Kuwait in 1991 and the devastating impact of this on the home countries' economies. Remittances also induce a level of insecurity due to the way they bypass the state and strengthen non-state actors. This is why regimes have recently tried to exert ever more control over them by imposing restrictions on currency transfers and bank withdrawals. What is undeniable is that in Jordan, migrant remittances contributed a large share of the GDP and have thus benefited society at large and helped to raise the general welfare level.

* * *

Revenues that accrued directly to the state, in contrast to the situation in Iraq, were not spent on militarization but redistributed and allocated to strategic groups, thereby creating new rentier alliances (Knowles 2005). The Jordanian state incorporated strategically important social groups and sectors into the state apparatus and employed a strategy whereby political legitimacy was achieved through the allocation of public resources. This is similar to strategies of state making employed in the rentier states of the Gulf peninsula. In Jordan, the incorporation occurred primarily via employment in the state administration and in the public sector. Between 1970 and 1985 the number of civil servants grew by 300 percent (Jreisat 1989: 98–99). Welfare meant public-sector employment with attendant benefits for the entire family; along with a steady income, these jobs provided access to healthcare and cheap consumer goods. By the early 1980s, civilian employment in the state bureaucracy reached around 47 percent of employment (Baylouny 2008) and thereby attained the same importance as a source of employment as the army had done during the mandate era. In 1997, military employment reached ten percent of the labor force and is some rural areas this even reached 20 percent.

Four groups in particular were incorporated into the state: Jordanian landowners, the financial and commercial bourgeoisie of Palestinian origin, parts of the educated middle class, and the Bedouins (Schwarz 2004: 24–28). The state created large settlement programs based on irrigation schemes, thereby cultivating its legitimation of Bedouin heritage and creating jobs in the state administration linked to water allocation.[3] Finally, incorporation of social groups into the state also occurred via the assignment of members of the Palestinian elite to senior positions in the ministries of agriculture, economics, education, development, and foreign affairs (Mishal 1980). These appointments came particularly after Israel's annexation of the West Bank in 1949 and demonstrate that the Hashemite regime trusted Palestinians, as a group, less than it did Bedouin tribal groups (Migdal 2001: 78). Indeed, when in September 1970 Palestinian groups challenged the Hashemite state, Jordan's army intervened against the less well equipped and less thoroughly trained PLO forces. The Syrian army intervened in support of the Palestinian forces and entered Jordanian territory from the north. King Hussein appealed for help to the United Kingdom and the United States, but questions of timing and terrain made it clear that only the Israeli military could effectively intervene. Thus was born the U.S. plan for direct military involvement. Even this the threatened regime was prepared to accept in extremis. As it happened, open Israeli moves toward the north in preparation for intervention were sufficient to give the Syrians pause. When the Hashemite regime, assured by outside support, finally committed its air force against Syrian ground troops, Syria's own air force did not intervene.[4] This episode in state making highlighted the fragility of the Jordanian state. It was only outside intervention that stopped the crisis from leading to state failure. But this episode also highlighted the fact that domestic alliances could lead to stability or breed instability. Especially, a move toward Palestinians as a new base of support could create instability and entail the daunting challenge of redefining the country's national identity. The real centers of state power—the offices of the prime minister, the minister of interior, and the army—have from then on remained in the hands of tribal-group members and largely closed to Palestinians.[5]

While conscription into the army was occasionally used to bolster the regime's legitimacy, the higher echelons within the force remained in the hands of loyal Bedouins (Mishal 1980: 177; Migdal 2001).

Today, Jordan can be characterized as an institutionally weak state that relies not on domestic resource extraction, but on external rents. Yet Jordan also possesses characteristics that compensate for this frailty through state-provided welfare, thereby forging the building of a strong nation. The social origins of Jordan and the attachment of key social groups to the state through material benefits date back to the mandate era. Not blessed like Iraq with abundant oil revenues, Jordan had to earn its rent revenues and consequently was less tempted to overspend revenue on military capacity. A key factor in Jordan's avoidance of state failure has been this social contract. While projecting stability, it does not indicate state strength, nor does it guarantee absolute domestic control. It is a bargain that has to be negotiated over time. Especially during times of declining revenues, when economic boom turns to bust and overspending threatens fiscal crises, this contract comes into question. Austerity measures demand cutbacks in welfare benefits and entitlements and occasionally lead to protest. The fuel riots that occurred in Ma'an in 1989 and the bread riots in Karak in 1996 constitute political signals that point toward a change in the social contract brought about by the economic situation. They also point to a neglect of certain groups or regions in terms of the state's distribution policies (Tell 2000: 17). The linkage between welfare and representation has to be constantly re-negotiated (Brand 1992). The prime considerations in this context become budget security (Brand 2001), the acquisition of new rents, and the maintenance of the state's allocative power in the face of weak infrastructural power. Institutions of statehood do exist but serve the purpose of allocation, patronage, and distribution of welfare (Kilani and Sakijha 2000). They are informal in nature and describe tacit social rules that structure social, economic, and political interactions. The use of the term "informal" makes no judgment on the legal or non-legal nature of the rules, but highlights the point that while institutions may seem similar, they function differently. In all this, the Jordanian experience of state making differs from the European one.

Jordan as a Rentier State

Extractive capacity is a necessary prerequisite for states to fulfill their welfare function. Rentier states, as I have shown in Chapter 1, have the luxury of not having to revert to direct taxation; they can rely on rent revenues to finance their domestic spending policies and welfare commitments. Jordan exemplifies this situation. The country receives large amounts of foreign military and development aid. This leads to a transnationalization of state making. Jordan's "persistent success in securing sizeable amounts of foreign economic assistance" distinguishes it from its neighbors (Askari, Cummings, and Glover 1982: 272–73). Economic aid has exceeded domestic revenues nearly every year for the past 30 years. This has allowed a spending policy similar to that of rentier states. Indeed, in 1977 Jordan was world leader in terms of obtaining economic aid, being exceeded only by Bangladesh; other Arab states receiving aid, such as Egypt, Syria, Lebanon, or Tunisia, were clearly ranked below Jordan (ibid.: 274).

Jordan's extractive capacity relies on both direct and indirect taxes, amounting to 18 percent in 1951, to 21 percent in 1954, and to 25 percent in 1962. During this period government spending was more than double the overall revenue level; this was largely possible only due to the influx of strategic rents (see table 3.2). During the 1960s and 1970s, revenues obtained via domestic taxation dropped again, reaching 12.4 percent in 1966, 11.8 percent in 1968, 11.6 percent in 1970, 13.6 in 1972, 17.9 in 1976, and 13.5 in 1978 (ibid.: 149). Despite the increased capacities of the Jordanian state to generate domestic sources of revenue, foreign assistance grew equally during the same period; up to 1978 it matched domestic extraction. More importantly, and despite the overall increase in domestic taxation (in absolute terms and not in relation to foreign assistance), the composition of these taxes remained the same. Customs duties and other consumption excises accounted for about half of all revenues, while income taxes accounted for only around 12 percent. A comparison between overall domestic revenue extraction and deliveries of overall foreign aid (excluding military aid) demonstrated Jordan's exceptional characteristic: a state that succeeded

Table 3.2. Rent revenues in Jordan (as percentage of total revenues)

1921	1931	1941	1967	1970	1973	1979	1981	1982	1994	1995	1997
50	34	43	57	48.7	40	44.9	33.4	30.5	44	47.7	42.7

Sources: Amawi (1993: 275); Central Bank of Jordan (1999); Tell (2000: 185); Robins (2004: 143).

in securing sizeable amounts of strategic rents. Where the state did levy taxes, it did so in the socially least disruptive manner possible: via indirect taxation. Direct taxes were applied only to middle-income families employed within the state bureaucracy. The fiscal history of Jordan thus demonstrates how large amounts of strategic rents created rent-seeking behavior.

Economic aid helped to maintain a system of allocation, with distribution channels running throughout society, in rural areas to a particularly pronounced degree (Kingston 1996). Such channels included institutions for aid allocation, strong tribal affiliations, strong informal personal ties, and the omnipresence of *wasta* ("intercession, mediation"—the social mechanism that determines allocation decisions) in the public sector and the state administration (Kilani and Sakijha 2000, 2002). The absence of uniform procedures regarding the hiring of civil servants led to the manipulation of politics and the prevalence of personalized relationships. However, economic aid was dependent on outside donors—the United States, the United Kingdom, and the oil-exporting Gulf states—so was volatile. It had to be compensated for by developing social cohesion and a sense of selfhood among the population. In this context the relevance of tribes, tribalism, and wider ethnic identity became part of state- and nation-building via education and welfare programs (Bocco 1989; Salamé 1994: 7–32). While a territorial understanding of statehood clashed initially with existing identity structures, a new, common national identity was fostered. This was adapted by the new state elites and by nascent state-builders; it was particularly pronounced in Jordan compared with other states in the Middle East.

Legitimacy and Political Rule

The legitimacy of Jordan's monarchs traditionally rests on the ancestry of the Hashemites as descendants of the Prophet Muhammad, the projection of their role as defenders of Islamic holy places, and as the instigators and leaders of the great Arab Revolt against the Ottomans. The Hashemite claim to political rule in Jordan was finalized in 1991, when the late King Hussein united all social forces to sign up to the National Charter (al-Mithaq al-Watani), which set out in Article 1 that Jordan's system of political rule would be Hashemite and dynastic. Since 2005, a new pattern of legitimacy based on economic performance has been employed by King Abdullah II—Hussein's son and successor as head of state. Legitimacy now stresses economic liberalization in order to maintain state welfare. After the economic distress of the 1990s, which had started with a fiscal crisis in 1989, Jordan had to implement structural economic reforms. Declining budget allocations meant less money for key social groups. To compensate for this, the regime promoted a modernization of the Jordanian economy. This was to be achieved by accession to the World Trade Organization (achieved in 2005), by signing free-trade agreements (one such was signed with the United States in 2000), and through domestic economic policies and reforms. Moves included the establishment of advisory councils; one such was the Economic Consultative Council (ECC), set up in December 1999. The ECC served as an influential policy-formulation body and gained the reputation of functioning as a parallel government (Schlumberger and Bank 2002: 57). The ECC was used as a way of overcoming resistance to economic reform from within the conservatively oriented elites—especially the state bureaucracy, the security sector, and Bedouins (Bank and Schlumberger 2004: 42; Milton-Edwards and Hinchcliffe 1999).[6] Legitimacy also included prioritization of public diplomacy initiatives, such as the hosting of the World Economic Forum at the Dead Sea. The re-emphasis on economic issues dominated Jordanian public discourse and sidelined other issues such as democratic reform (which had been omnipresent in the 1990s). The economy was now prioritized, to the detriment of political and democratic reforms;

it was claimed the latter needed to be postponed until the population at large could benefit from economic reforms.

The reality looked rather different. Accession to the World Trade Organization and the free-trade agreement with the United States did create several thousand jobs among qualified individuals in industry (P. Moore 2004).[7] Nevertheless, unemployment remained high—at an estimated 20 percent—and population growth continued rapidly, with per-capita income remaining locked at its 1984 level (P. Moore 2003). Jordan did succeed in bolstering its image and its legitimacy abroad. At the time EU trade commissioner Pascal Lamy publicly declared Jordan to be "a fine regional example" and "a pathfinder for the whole region" (Jordan Times, 24 June 2003). Jordan also became a reliable partner in the U.S.-initiated "War against Terror"; Jordan received US$700 million from the United States for its role in the 2003 Iraq war (P. Moore 2003). Jordan served as the main gateway to Iraq, and most of the money for Iraqi reconstruction was channeled through Jordan. Thanks in part to U.S. aid and along with increased business opportunities in the transportation and tourism sector, Jordan's per-capita income grew to US$2,000; this created economic stability and enabled the continuation of state welfare. At the same time, Jordan did have to handle the socio-economic consequences of the influx of half a million of Iraqi refugees; Jordan managed this with the help of aid received from abroad.

However, the actual politics of the Jordanian regime in relation to respecting political liberties and human rights stood in contrast to the image of a liberal and open state. The geopolitical situation following 9/11 helped perpetuate this situation. The absence of any fundamental U.S. critique of the domestic political behavior of certain regimes that were deemed to be strategic partners for Washington in the War against Terror represented a chance for a clampdown on political dissidents (Economist, 27 October 2001). The geopolitical situation allowed regimes to combat any domestic political dissent in the name of the fight against terror. In Jordan, for example, the penal code was amended to allow the introduction of anti-terror regulations and a tightening of press restrictions, with jail terms imposed for slandering the monarchy and for writings that were seen as undermining national security (Financial Times, 16 January 2002; Amnesty International 2002). Although these measures turned out to be temporary, many Jordanians saw them as an illustration of how the U.S.-led anti-terror campaign was misused to allow the introduction of additional restrictions on public freedom, and certainly as a sign of the security forces' increased influence over political life. Further limitations in the public sphere came in 2009, when King Abdullah dismissed parliament with no date for new elections being scheduled.

To be clear, this de-liberalization trend did not begin with the events of 9/11 (Bank and Schlumberger 2004; Schwedler 2002). After the 1994 peace treaty with Israel, the Jordanian government reasserted control over the public sphere, silencing critics and discouraging public debates on sensitive topics (Lynch 2002: 35). In 1997 the government passed a law that resulted in the closure of most of the independent weekly press, marking a clear break with the early 1990s, when there was openness in the public sphere. In the same year the regime initiated a crackdown on the Palestinian organization Hamas in order to reinforce the image of Jordan as a Jordanian and not a Palestinian state. The new image was echoed in Jordanian-Palestinian relations, where on numerous occasions King Abdullah asserted that "Jordan supports without reservation the creation of a Palestinian state" and "there is no such word as confederation in my vocabulary" (ibid.: 46). Even with regard to the issue of Jerusalem, King Abdullah renounced a Jordanian role in the administration of the Islamic sites. This rhetoric was met with selected policies, such as the passing of a citizenship law in December 2002, thereby effectively avoiding Jordan's conversion into a Hashemite Palestine, as well as Jordan's foreign-policy decision to side with the United States in the war against Iraq in 2003, and finally repeated Jordanian participation in the initiatives to re-launch the Middle East peace process. All these policies were in line with the Jordanian state's interest in balancing its international role as a reliable partner of the United States and as the principal Arab mediator in the Middle East conflict, with its domestic security concern being to pacify its Palestinian population by taking an active lead in resolving the conflict through the establishment of a viable Palestinian state.

*　*　*

State making in Jordan clearly showed a linkage between the welfare function and the representation function of the state. This translated into changing debates about the priority of political reform or national identity. In the years following independence in 1946, debates about whether Jordan should be the homeland of Palestinians or be a Jordanian state were prominent. After Black September in 1970—when the conflict between Palestinian guerrilla groups and the Jordanian authorities led to the PLO's expulsion to Lebanon—this debate was politically and militarily decided in favor of a Jordanian state; henceforth, the East Bank was indeed such a state. In 1991 it was further decided that Jordan would also be a Hashemite state, as laid down in the National Charter. With the fiscal crisis in 1988 and 1989, state revenues declined, leading to the state's withdrawal from its welfare function. The fiscal crisis of the Jordanian rentier state caused the debate on national identity to shift toward political issues and saw the restart of parliamentary elections in 1989. After a decade of political liberalization and the death of King Hussein in 1999, the state again retreated from its representation function and shifted public debate to the economic realm and to achieving prosperity through development. With the regional agenda shifting after 9/11, debates about national identity were again changed and now forged in terms of national security. This saw a securitization of the public debate. Jordan portrayed itself as an island of stability in a region of instability. Internal cohesion and national unity were key factors in maintaining this. The national debates al-'Urdun 'Auwallan ("Jordan First") and Kulluna al-'Urdun ("We Are All Jordan") are concrete examples. State making was under way. As with the National Pact at the beginning of the 1990s, when the nature of the Jordanian regime was debated, King Abdullah invited representatives of all sectors of Jordanian society to unite and to agree on the nature of Jordanian statehood (Jordan Times, 13 July 2006).

Security concerns are at the top of the agenda, given the instability in neighboring Iraq, the rise of Islamist terrorism, the terrorist threat in Jordan (there were hotel bombings in November 2005), and regional insecurity (the Middle East conflict). At the moment of writing, security concerns are influencing the dimensions of Jordanian state making and national identity. To a large degree the state has forged the debates and the directions of national identity, whether away from welfare concerns or toward security issues. In all instances this has been driven by regional concerns. Jordan has remained reactionary and has not pursued an active policy aimed at influencing regional conditions, but reacted (arguably successfully) to it. National identity in Jordan remains multifaceted and fuzzy (Frisch 2002; Shyrock 2000). It includes several dimensions, among them an Islamic dimension, an Arab dimension, and a tribal dimension. The unifying point of reference for state making has remained the Arab Revolt of 1916. The many dimensions of Jordanian national identity are amenable according to political situation: when it comes to the Palestinian issue, the Islamic dimension becomes prominent; when it comes to developments in Iraq, the Arab dimension becomes prominent; and when it comes to Bedouin affairs, the tribal dimension receives attention. All in all, the state can to a large degree forge a national identity and thereby compensate for weaknesses in the fulfillment of its core functions.

*　*　*

Jordan clearly defies the "war-makes-states" theory, which would predict the emergence of a strong state. The opposite is the case: Jordan shows clear elements of institutional weakness of the state in the domains of representation and welfare, similarly to Iraq prior to the 1990 invasion of Kuwait. While Jordan managed to avoid state failure as in Iraq, it has remained characterized by weak statehood. Hence, Jordan offers an intriguing case for explaining state survival in the face of fragility. For much of Jordan's history the state has been in real peril of being wiped off the map. Yet the Jordanian monarchy has proven to be one of the most resilient in the Middle East and the threat of state extinction is no longer present. Contributing to Jordan's survival has been the availability of rents, the loyalty of the armed forces, and the consistent interest of external powers in Jordan's continued stability. All this has been facilitated by financial resources made available to Jordan's rulers through foreign rents. Rentierism has thereby contributed to the survival of the Jordanian state in that it has allowed generous welfare allocation to key social groups and a high degree of militarization which has strengthened the military establishment.

Jordan's example of state making shows how semi-rentier states broadly follow the path of state making set by oil states, as the history of the United Arab Emirates and the other Gulf states shows. Jordan is characterized as an infrastructurally weak state that relies not on domestic resource extraction but on external rents (development aid, strategic rents and migrant remittances). Jordan compensates for this weakness via state-provided welfare, thereby promoting state- and nation-building. While the Jordanian state did create institutions and impose control over its own territory, it did not succeed in full democratization and the "civilianization of government and domestic politics" (Tilly 1990: 206). Today Jordan is not a liberal democracy, although it displays some elements of political legitimacy and its political system is relatively free and open. But a pure logic of war- and state making cannot explain this, nor can it explain the longevity of the Jordanian state, as the latter is weak yet continues to survive. This chapter has argued that rentierism is central in explaining state making in Jordan. Were it not for the availability of external rents, many fragile states like Jordan would probably have succumbed to institutional state collapse, even while maintaining a legal façade of statehood. Jordan did not suffer extinction at the hands of larger states and was not exposed to a brutal competitive international state system as in early modern Europe; more importantly, Jordan used its rents for the incorporation of social groups into the regime and not for war making. The combination of rentierism and war making in today's world thus produces a twin phenomenon of state failure and the breakdown of the rentier state, as in the case of Iraq, and life support for fragile states, as in Jordan.

4

The Gulf States
From Tribal Sheikhdoms to Sustainable States

Oil put this state, together with some of its oil-producing neighbors, on the international map. It serves as a bridge for contacts with the rest of the world.

Frauke Heard-Bey, *From Trucial States to United Arab Emirates*

The United Arab Emirates and the other small Gulf states (Kuwait, Bahrain and Qatar) stand in contrast to Iraq and Jordan: no Gulf state has been engaged in war making since independence.[1] The history of state making within the United Arab Emirates shows that oil revenues have produced sustainable statehood in the absence of war making and militarization;[2] the state embarked on economic diversification during the oil-boom years and set in place a policy of capital acquisition based on the attraction of foreign direct investment, and in this way a sustainable rentier structure was created. Welfare provisions in the United Arab Emirates have today become sustainable to the point that even during periods of low world oil prices the state is still able to fulfill its commitments. The United Arab Emirates and the other small Gulf states have undergone state making without the experience of war making and have changed from tribal sheikhdoms into sustainable rentier states with embedded authority structures. The states are small and in need of great-power support, but they have managed their survival.

War and State Making in the Gulf States

The United Arab Emirates was created in December 1971, when the group of six Emirates formerly known as the Trucial States obtained independence from the United Kingdom.[3] The emergence of modern states in the Gulf region was closely linked with the United Kingdom's role (Joyce 2003). Since the middle of the seventeenth century the British had shown a strategic interest in the region, aiming first to secure trade with India against piracy in the area, then to protect the sea route to India via the Suez Canal and the port of Aden. In 1763 the English East India Company established an office in Bushehr (Kelly 1968). At the beginning of the nineteenth century the United Kingdom extended its reach into the Gulf through diplomatic relations. Maritime truces were agreed with local rulers in 1819, 1820, 1835 and 1853. These treaties were crucial for the future path toward statehood, since they established which tribal sheikhs would be considered independent rulers. It was generally those rulers with whom the British had concluded maritime agreements who later found their way to rulership of a sovereign state. These rulers were the sheikhs of Abu Dhabi, Dubai, Sharjah, 'Ajman and 'Umm al-Quwain. Later in the nineteenth century Ra's al-Khaimah split from Sharjah, increasing the number of independent Trucial States to six. The only exception was the territory of Qawasim, which was never recognized by the United Kingdom as an independent entity and hence never included within the United Arab Emirates as a sovereign state (Walker 1994: vi–vii).

*   *   *

State consolidation in the United Arab Emirates was driven by three factors: the recognition of tribal leaders by the United Kingdom, with those so recognized later becoming sovereign rulers; early manifestations of sovereignty, such as the collection of taxes and the application of jurisdiction; and the decentralized control of tribal society through trusted persons (sons or brothers of ruling sheikhs) and through representatives (*walis*). The maritime truce of 1835 and the permanent truce of 1853 were concluded between the United Kingdom and the rulers of Sharjah, Dubai, 'Ajman and Abu Dhabi. In March 1892 these same states plus 'Umm al-Quwain agreed on behalf of themselves and their successors "not to enter into any agreement or correspondence with any Power other than the British Government." This exclusive agreement bound the states in terms of foreign and military policies not to "cede, sell, mortgage or otherwise give for occupation any part of territory except to the British Government" (Heard-Bey 1996: 293; Crystal 1990).[4] In 1922, this agreement was reconfirmed and extended to cover oil policy, with an agreement not to give oil concessions to any company which was not supported by the British government. While the monopoly over external relations lay clearly with the United Kingdom following the agreements of 1892 and 1922, the British government tried to avoid entanglement in the domestic affairs of the Trucial States prior to World War II by supporting the actual and claimed rulers over the tribes in the interior of the country. The Trucial rulers were able to affirm their authority—in theory and practice—much more easily in the absence of foreign interference and at times even with active outside support. This was conducive to effective state making; it stood in stark contrast to the blocked attempts at state making in other parts of the Middle East during the mandate era, such as in Iraq, Jordan, Syria, or Palestine. After World War II the United Kingdom reverted to a much more active policy with regard to the internal and external affairs of the Trucial States, but without hampering the nascent process of state making. The very decision that led to the creation of the United Arab Emirates was entirely an external one, on the part of the United Kingdom. In February 1967 the Labor government of Harold Wilson decided, for purely domestic reasons relating to the financial burden of Britain's colonial military bases, to publish a White Paper announcing the closure of all military bases east of Suez and British withdrawal from the region prior to the end of 1971. It was only the tight withdrawal schedule that accelerated negotiations among the Trucial States themselves to form a federation; this was initially envisaged as including nine states, including Bahrain and Qatar. After a series of six top-level meetings between the ruling sheikhs between May 1968 and October 1969, agreement on the planned federation neared; however, eventually the federation failed to emerge because Bahrain and Qatar declared independence unilaterally, in August and September 1971 respectively. The remaining emirates formed the United Arab Emirates on 2 December 1971.

The domestic exercise of authority in pre-independence United Arab Emirates included levying taxes (Heard-Bey 1996: 113). Important taxes included those linked to the pearling industry, agricultural products, the system of licensing fishing rights, and the 2.5 percent customs duty levied at the major ports along the coast. Taxes were collected via agents of the rulers, via salaried and armed tribesman, or in the case of customs duties, via merchants. The fact that customs duties were collected by merchants strengthened the influence of the latter within the political system, as rulers would often turn to them for financial assistance in years when the other sources of revenues did not suffice. Thus a domestic social contract was installed that accounted for power-sharing and political checks—as for example in 1938–39 (Al-Sayegh 1998: 90). Manifestations of political authority also included the distribution of benefits. The payments of subsidies by a ruler to a tribe, the administration and application of jurisdiction, and the provision of common goods were concrete manifestations of legitimate, sovereign rule. Especially the practice of administering jurisdiction highlights how sovereign rule was linked to legitimate rule: as jurisdiction had to be requested by a plaintiff (simply adjudicating for the sake of law did not exist), both parties had to accept the judge, the law, and eventually the verdict. The legal principles that guided this process (third-party arbitration and customary law) went beyond strictly legal script, as judgments could include considerations about who could and hence would pay costs (Heard-Bey 1996: 113).

The administration of government affairs in a tribal society demonstrates the specificity of state making in the United Arab Emirates. Indeed, Western concepts of nation-state, territorial boundaries, and sovereignty were largely alien to the society in question. Tribal politics first and foremost concerned authority over people and not over territory.[5] Problems arose, as tribal affiliation was not permanent and tribes could change alliances between rulers. Individual exit strategies existed symbolically: one could transfer one's allegiance to another ruler or do so geographically by moving to another community. However, such options were restricted in reality by the precedence of the community over the individual, so it was rare for a whole community to shift its allegiance.[6] Questions of tribal loyalty led to violent inter-tribal clashes which at times turned into wars.[7] As tribal custom relied on mediation and accommodation, gaining neighboring tribes as allies became perhaps as important as the actual fighting itself, since the latter often consisted only of occasional raids on enemy villages and did not cause human casualties exceeding single figures. Tensions in the hinterland of the Trucial States became more pronounced with the worldwide economic depression of the 1930s, at which time the interior fell into what was almost a "state of constant warfare" (Heard-Bey 1996: 302). In September 1945 increasingly hostile relationships turned into a war between the two large emirates of Dubai and Abu Dhabi, over the exact demarcation of their territories. Early 1948 saw 52 members of the Manasir tribe killed—and the previous custom whereby human casualties would be kept low was broken. The population became apprehensive of the war and popular opinion swung in favor of a peaceful settlement, which eventually came at the hands of the British authorities. Political rule, in short, extended through personal relationships and proximity to individuals, groups and families, irrespective of where the latter resided. Exact borders were not demarcated, remaining informal (Al-Naqeeb 1990). Disputes about demarcations of internal territorial boundaries were nevertheless (perhaps because of the uncertainty) a common feature within the Trucial States.

The discovery of and further exploration for oil in the aftermath of World War II brought territorial issues to even greater prominence. In 1945, a three-year war began between Abu Dhabi and Dubai, over a territorial dispute. In 1952 another territorial dispute erupted, this time over control over the Buraimi oasis in the Rub' al-Khali desert. Representatives of Saudi Arabia arrived at the oasis in August 1952 and claimed it as Saudi territory. In 1933 King 'Abdulaziz of Saudi Arabia had signed a petroleum concession with Standard Oil of California that extended exploration rights to the eastern portion of the Saudi kingdom. As these frontiers were not specified exactly, questions arose about the exact demarcation of Saudi territory for purposes of future oil exploration and production. The British government considered the so-called "Blue Line" to be Saudi Arabia's eastern frontier. This line had been agreed at the convention of 1913–14 between the United Kingdom and the Ottoman Empire, and as Saudi Arabia represented a successor state to the Ottoman Empire in that region, it was held that the convention continued to apply. However, in 1953 the Saudi representatives based their claim on the fact that the tribes of the oasis had paid the religious tax (*zakat*) for decades and thereby accepted Saudi sovereignty and authority (Kelly 1956). There was opposition from Abu Dhabi, however, and a long period of diplomatic negotiation ensued, which led to the submission of the case to an international arbitration panel in July 1954.[8] However, by 1955 international arbitration had collapsed. The United Kingdom decided to side with Abu Dhabi and send the Trucial Oman Scouts—a small, British-led police force created to pacify the interior of Oman—to expel the Saudi representatives from Buraimi.[9] The dispute was settled de facto in 1955 when the Saudi contingent left the oasis; however, no de jure settlement was signed. A de jure agreement was reached in 1974, but is still awaiting ratification from the United Arab Emirates and Saudi Arabia.[10] Another formally unsettled territorial dispute related to the border with Oman; this was eventually delineated in May 1999, but again there was no judicial settlement.

The history of the modern Gulf states is characterized by these kinds of territorial dispute. As most of the population is concentrated in the coastal areas, the state and its institutions came to be concentrated there to the detriment of the tribal hinterland. Prior to the mid-twentieth century none of the Trucial States extended its political control to the interior—for geographical reasons, namely the inaccessibility of the Rub' al-Khali desert. For the same reason, the Royal Navy did not extend its reach beyond coastal areas and left tribal quarrels in the hinterland to local mediation. Only in the 1950s did the United Kingdom become involved in these internal territorial disputes, as an arbiter. The local rulers, with the exception of Sheikh Shakhbut of Abu Dhabi, accepted that British political agents would arbitrate on borders between the Trucial States, including the contested areas between Sharjah and Dubai, and Fujairah and Ra's al-Khaimah in the mountains.[11] In 1956 and 1957 the first of these boundaries awards were made, with little objection from the rulers concerned. Grotesquely, this included the division of the territories of Sharjah into six separate parts, Ajman into three, and Ra's al-Khaimah, Dubai and Fujairah into two parts each; the resulting patchwork bears some resemblance to the map of early modern Europe. But while the rulers of the Trucial States did agree to accept the Western concept of fixed boundaries, this did not mean, as one British official put it, that they also accepted "our ideas of neatness and logicality" (Walker 1994: x). The overlap of territories produced, in the long run, a logic that was conducive to unification and state making. Occasional disputes over territories did occur after the creation of the United Arab Emirates,[12] but in no case has the concept of a single country united via a federation of seven emirates been seriously questioned.

*   *   *

State making in the United Arab Emirates demonstrates further specific characteristics beyond the points about being a patchwork of internal territories and about unsettled external territorial issues. With the challenges of globalization, traditional elements of authority have been merged (Rizvi 1993; Heard-Bey 2005). At the beginning of the twenty-first century the United Arab Emirates became the hub for regional trade in the Middle East. For the everyday traveler to the United Arab Emirates the country's experience of state building is felt immediately, via the magnitude and rapidity of the growth of the state: what were small villages in the desert have grown into large metropolitan cities. In the United Arab Emirates, as in the Gulf more generally, recent decades have witnessed the development of a close relationship between rulers and merchants (Al-Sayegh 1998). Rulers made land available to those who collected debts for them. The buying and selling of land for public-development projects at inflated prices was an important way of allocating resources. Another method was to receive business contracts from the government, licenses for production, and imports, or to ensure a domestic monopoly. This is characteristic of a neopatrimonial regime and demonstrates how the state apparatus is run like an enterprise. Dubai is at the forefront of these developments.

Historically, Dubai was a harbor from which small and medium-sized boats sailed to other parts of the Gulf region and to the Indian subcontinent and east Africa in order to trade in pearls, foodstuffs, and textiles. Taxes on pearling boats were imposed and merchants contributed large amounts to rulers' revenues. A domestic fiscal bargain emerged. In the 1930s a reform movement pushed for greater participation in the political and economic affairs of the sheikhdom. The attempt to bring the paternalistic and authoritarian structure of tribal society into harmony with the structure of a multinational merchant society led to the establishment of a parliamentary council (Majlis) in October 1938. The agreement which the ruler of Dubai had to sign stipulated that "the income and the expenditure of the state had to be spent in the name of the state and had to have the approval of the *Majlis*" (Heard-Bey 1996: 256). An allowance of one-eighth of the total revenue of Dubai was to be allocated to the ruler. However, this clause was never fully implemented and its contentious nature eventually led to the termination of the council in March 1939. The entire Majlis was dissolved by Sheikh Sa'id bin Maktum. It was replaced by the Majlis al-Tujjar, which was presided over by Sheikh Sa'id, consisted of appointed members, and served essentially as an advisory board on economic matters without budgetary oversight (Al-Sayegh 1998: 96).

*　*　*

Compared to these early attempts at creating a domestic political bargain from the existing economic structures of traders and merchants, more important for state making was the role of outside powers, particularly the United Kingdom. Trade and security became closely intertwined, as trade routes had to be protected against pirates and local rulers incorporated within the British system of indirect control. The initial policy of taking responsibility only for the external relations of the Trucial States was abandoned by the United Kingdom after World War II, with the British government eventually becoming actively involved in strengthening institutions of domestic governance. Separate armed forces had existed in the seven emirates since the eighteenth century, and these continued in existence even after the creation of the Trucial Oman Levies in 1951. In fact, the emirates' separate defense

Table 4.1. Comparison of military forces in the Gulf region

	UAE	Bahrain	Saudi Arabia	Oman	Qatar	Kuwait
Armed forces (total)	64,500	11,000	162,500	43,500	11,800	15,300
Reserve troops	—	—	20,000	—	—	23,700
Ground troops	59,000	8,500	127,000	31,500	8,500	11,000
Air forces	4,000	1,500	18,000	4,100	1,500	2,500
Naval forces	1,500	1,000	13,500	4,200	1,800	1,800

Source: Dar al-Khalij lil-sihafa wa al-thiba'a wa al-nashr, 2001 (author's translation).

establishments were supported in the 1960s by temporary transfers and contracting of British army officers (Heard-Bey 1996: 314).

Following independence, security concerns did not figure prominently on the state-making agenda of the newly created United Arab Emirates. Despite the United Kingdom's formal disappearance from the scene, that country remained the external guarantor of security (later the United States did too); this meant that domestic security configurations only emerged to a modest degree, and that later close cooperation with the United States, the provision of military facilities prior to the 1990–91 Iraq war, and several arms deals characterized the security function of the state (Cordesman 2004). The United Arab Emirates substituted its own provision of security for a de facto assurance that it would receive U.S. military assistance in the event of invasion by another state. While this externalization of security was purely defensive, no provision was made to actively seek solutions (for example, with Iran over the contested islands in the Gulf).[13] This demonstrated the limitations on the state's infrastructural power. The United Arab Emirates encountered political difficulties over extracting manpower for military and security purposes; today, about 30 percent of the United Arab Emirates' 64,000 active soldiers are expatriates. The state has one of the most technologically advanced armies in the region and participated in international peacekeeping operations in the Balkans, Somalia, and Afghanistan.

The United Arab Emirates' army is large in absolute terms compared with the armies of neighboring Arab states in the Gulf, as table 4.1 highlights. However, the total includes 15,000 men belonging to the

Table 4.2. UAE defense expenditure (in billion UAE dirhams, AED)

Year	Defense expenditure (total)	GDP	Percentage
1989	5.4	100.1	5.4
1990	9.51	124	7.7
1991	18	123.6	14.6
1992	7.7	128.4	6.0
1993	7.8	131.6	5.9
1994	7.8	137	5.7
1995	7.2	144	5.0
1996	7.6	158	4.8
1997	8.9	176	5.1
1998	11	170	6.5
1999	11.3	190	5.9
2000	11	213	5.2
2001	10.5	249	4.2
2002	10.5	261	4.0
2003	9.23	286	3.2
2004	9.49	328	2.9
2005	9.74	435	2.2

Source: Author's calculations based on IISS (various years). GDP figures for 2005 are estimates based on Economist Intelligence Unit 2005g.

armed forces of Dubai, which are not fully integrated into the United Arab Emirates' armed forces, so the overall size of the federal army is considerably smaller than 64,000. The technologically advanced equipment possessed by the United Arab Emirates' military is matched by the forces' operational abilities, but not by the level of resource extraction from society. Furthermore, the imbalance within the federation between Abu Dhabi and Dubai translates into the existence of separate military forces and only limited integrated structures. In the United Arab Emirates, the low level of militarization in terms of extraction of manpower and defense spending (per GDP) as well as the decentralization of armed forces stand out, as highlighted in table 4.2. The centralization and consolidation of the federal state has been hindered by the existence of separate armies, police forces, and court systems in the seven emirates.

The particularistic ambitions of each emirate existed only as long as external military threats, such as the 1979 Iranian Revolution and the

1980–88 Iran-Iraq War, were felt. In these times of insecurity a decision was taken to advance in terms of internal political centralization, as well as expansion of the federal administration financed by revenues from the largest emirate, Abu Dhabi. Additionally, an external security arrangement with the United States existed. This allowed for the continuous cultural identity of the different emirates and an extending state-building agenda attached to a slowly growing federal political identity under the "father figure" of Sheikh Zayed (Heard-Bey 2005: 365). Apart from the short-lived presence of indirect external threats at the beginning of the 1980s, the United Arab Emirates has followed a path of state making without war making, in contrast to the European model; in fact, it has been a path of rent-driven state making.

Oil and the Making of States

A hundred years ago few people would have taken any notice of the tribal chiefdoms of the Gulf. Today, the names of Saudi Arabia, Dubai and Abu Dhabi are commonly encountered in the international media, and the Gulf states play a key role in international relations. Oil exports and high oil prices placed the oil-producing states of the Gulf region on the international agenda. Oil came as a blessing to the Gulf states and made them wealthy when they were on the verge of bankruptcy owing to the collapse of the pearl trade on which they had previously depended for their livelihoods (Hay 1954: 443).

Oil played a crucial role in the emergence of the United Arab Emirates. After World War II, oil discoveries first put the United Arab Emirates, together with its oil-producing neighbors, on the international map and served as a bridge for contacts with the rest of the world (Heard-Bey 1996: 5). Territorial control of the tribal hinterland, the establishment of a state administration and the fixing of land and sea boundaries became important issues. Since then, oil wealth has allowed for the creation of infrastructure and for urban development, as well as for the creation of an extensive state apparatus. Oil revenue thereby produced a relatively effective state in the absence of war making, as the UAE regime embarked on economic diversification during the oil boom years and set in place a policy of resource and capital

Table 4.3. Oil dependence in the Gulf states, 1962–2006: Oil revenues as a percentage of total government revenue

Average	(1962–77)	(1995–2002)	(2002–6)
UAE	93%	55%	74%
Bahrain	67%	62%	68%
Kuwait	94%	66%	88%
Qatar	93%	68%	65%
Saudi Arabia	85%	74%	80%
Oman	95%	75%	76%
Total	88%	70%	75%

Sources: Figures for 1962–77 are from Waterbury (1997: 155). Where independence came after 1962, the figures start later. Figures for 1995–2002 are from Fasano (2003: 7) and figures from 2002–6 are the author's calculations, based on Bahrain (2006); Economist Intelligence Unit (2005c, 2005e, 2005g, 2005l); Kuwait (various years); Oman (various years); Qatar (2005), Saudi Arabia (2005), and UAE Central Bank (various years).

acquisition based on attracting foreign direct investment. The welfare provisions in the UAE rentier state have today become sustainable to the point that even during periods of declining natural resources (as in Dubai) or fiscal crisis (as in the 1980s or in 2007), the state is able to fulfill its welfare commitments. In creating a sustainable rentier structure, the United Arab Emirates managed to break the linkage between declining resources and rising demands for political participation. The United Arab Emirates thus handled oil wealth in a way conducive to state making. However, all this must be linked to domestic resource extraction if it is to produce lasting change and democratic governance structures. The situation in the other Gulf states is similar, as reliance on oil income is the key structural commonalty (see table 4.3).

Most of the Gulf states have pursued a rentier expenditure policy which included subsidies and a generous welfare system. This included subsidies on basic foodstuffs, free education, and healthcare, and a state bureaucracy as employer of last resort. Extensive social-welfare policies have led to a rigid expenditure structure which is difficult to reform and which makes it hard to diversify government revenues. In 2002 alone, welfare spending stood at 40 percent in Qatar, 60 percent in Kuwait and Oman, more than 60 percent in Saudi Arabia, and considerably more than 70 percent in the United Arab Emirates and Bahrain

Table 4.4. Comparison of defense expenditure in the Gulf region (as percentage of GDP)

Year	UAE	Bahrain	Saudi Arabia	Oman	Qatar	Kuwait
1989	5.4	4.7	17.7	16.2	—	6.6
1990	7.7	5.0	23.3	18.1	—	74.8
1991	14.6	5.5	32.5	14.5	14.0	141.8
1992	6.0	5.6	19.1	15.4	5.0	13.6
1993	5.9	5.5	13.1	16.7	4.3	13.0
1994	5.7	5.3	11.9	17.7	4.2	12.7
1995	5.0	5.4	13.7	16.9	9.7	12.5
1996	4.8	5.5	12.7	12.9	9.0	12.9
1997	5.1	6.0	12.4	12.3	13.6	12.0
1998	6.5	7.5	16.2	12.3	15.3	14.3
1999	5.9	7.5	15.3	10.8	9.9	11.1
2000	5.2	4.6	11.9	11.9	7.2	10.8
2001	4.2	4.3	14.0	14.3	9.4	9.9
2002	4.0	4.0	12.0	13.0	10.6	10.9
2003	3.2	4.8	8.7	11.3	9.9	9.7
2004	2.9	4.4	8.2	10.6	7.4	7.8

Source: Author's calculations based on IISS (various years).

(Fasano 2003: 7). In Oman and Saudi Arabia, defense spending figures were among the highest in the world; in 1998, these countries spent slightly more than 15 percent of GDP on the military, whereas other developing states such as Mexico and Indonesia spent only about 1 percent of GDP, with other oil-producing states such as Malaysia, Norway, or Venezuela spending only about 3 percent (Noreng 2004: 13). Although defense spending decreased by 2004 to around 8 percent for Saudi Arabia and 11 percent for Oman, the figures are still above the regional average. The United Arab Emirates and the other small Gulf states have spent considerably less on militarization (see table 4.4) and have concentrated rentier spending on welfare benefits.

Despite their considerable dependence on volatile oil revenues, few Gulf states adopted a budgetary policy in a medium-term framework aimed at de-linking public expenditure decisions from the evolution of short-term oil prices (Fasano 2003: 7). The diversification of government revenues and the development of non-oil activities progressed only modestly and did not generate corresponding non-oil revenues.

This is due to the non-tax revenue base of oil states, described in the first chapter. Tax exemptions are rampant and there are constant delays in adopting a modern tax system. Personal income taxes are not levied and taxation is applied only modestly on company profits. For example, Qatar has no personal income tax. Throughout much of the country's history as an independent state its tax system has been based on a pre-independence law promulgated in 1954 by the then British Foreign Minister, Anthony Eden. This law was supplanted through Decree Law No. 11 of 14 July 1993, which introduced a new income-tax law. The law envisaged the taxation of business profits, but exempted enterprises owned entirely by Qataris and, in the case of a joint ownership, the share of the Qatari nationals. It is, in short, a tax on foreigners. Furthermore, the effect of the progressive tax on company profits of 1993 is mitigated by a five-year tax holiday applied to new firms, by being applied only to foreign-owned firms, and by excluding any shares owned by Qatari nationals in mixed companies as well as any military contract.[14] Similar arrangements exist in the other Gulf states. The absence of a ruler-subject struggle over the financial revenues of the state set the Gulf states apart from European states. Table 4.5 shows that taxation plays only a minor role in revenue generation and where it does play a role this is based on taxation of foreigners or foreign-based companies. The domestic effect of taxation is thereby minimized. Despite various modifications to the structure of the tax system, this basic feature of rentier states has not changed. In 2002, non-oil revenues made up only 5 percent of non-oil GDP in Qatar, a mere 9 percent in Bahrain and Saudi Arabia, 10 percent in Kuwait and the United Arab Emirates, and 15 percent in Oman (Fasano 2003: 9). Had it not been for oil revenues, all Gulf states would have had large fiscal deficits.

The rentier states of the Gulf have become aware of their structural limitations and weaknesses and have opted for equal tax treatment of foreign and local companies in order to attract foreign investment and to diversify the base of state revenues. In Oman, for example, prudent utilization of oil revenues during boom years and investment in the development of social and physical infrastructure (health, transportation, water supply) have contributed to a diversification of the economic foundations of the state and to a stable path of state building (Mansur and Treichel 1999). In Bahrain, in June 2007 the authorities began to deduct a monthly 1 percent payroll tax to finance an unemployment benefits scheme. This provoked widespread complaints from workers and trade unions. Nevertheless, the government continued in its bid to diversify domestic resources and in November 2009 added another tax, on property purchases. However, despite some institutional reforms aimed at diversifying countries' economies and the revenue base of the state, the rentier nature of the Gulf states has not substantially changed over the last decade. Nevertheless, rentierism has consolidated states in the absence of war making and has produced stable regimes and embedded authority structures.

*   *   *

Oil has played a crucial role in this. After World War II a renewed strategic interest on the part of external actors emerged in the Gulf. The United Kingdom, as the patron and protector of the Trucial States, cared little about control of the tribal hinterland. But with oil exploration and oil profits in the offing, territorial control became important. Local rulers were asked to facilitate access to oilfields by foreign oil companies. This meant local rulers had to pay tribal leaders in order to assuage them: in this way, the rulers of Sharjah and Ra's al-Khaimah resumed responsibility over the tribes of Bani Qitab, Khawatir, and Ghafala, which had previously considered themselves independent. However, in the case of Fujairah the strategy of buying control and territorial authority did not succeed; this led to the recognition of the emirate as an independent Trucial State in 1951 (Walker 1994). In 1939, Abu Dhabi granted an oil concession to the British Iraq Petroleum Company, which created a subsidiary for oil exploration.[15] Within the United Arab Emirates, oil was discovered in Abu Dhabi in 1958 and the production and export of oil began in 1962. Initially, Abu Dhabi's oil production reached 6 million barrels a year, of which 5 million barrels were exported. This provided an estimated £706,000 of additional revenues for the Abu Dhabi government in 1962 alone. By the end of the decade Abu Dhabi's oil revenues reached £96,998,000 and oil production an annual 284 million barrels; of these, 31 million were produced in Dubai, where the production and export of oil started in September

Table 4.5. Tax systems in the Gulf states

Tax rates	Bahrain	Kuwait
Individuals		
a. nationals	None	None
b. foreigners (self-employed)	None	None
Corporate income		
a. local companies	None	None
b. oil companies	46 percent	55 percent
c. foreign companies	None, except foreign banks (fee)	Progressive tax structure (5–55 percent)
Customs duties	5 percent (most products); 0 percent (food); 100 percent (alcohol and tobacco)	5 percent (most products); 0 percent (food); 100 percent (alcohol and tobacco)
Export duties	None	4 percent on all goods not subject to import duties
Social security contributions	10 percent (employer), 5 percent (employee)	10 percent (employer), 5 percent (employee)
Other taxes	10 percent (municipal tax), 2 percent (training levy)	0.5 percent (property tax), 5 percent (obligatory donation to research)
Tax and other incentives	Direct subsidies on electricity, water and sewage	Tax holidays (up to 10 years); customs duty exemptions (imports of capital equipment and raw materials)

Source: Adapted from Fasano (2003: 47).

Oman	Qatar	Saudi Arabia	UAE
None	None	None	None
None	None	Progressive tax structure (from 5 to 30 percent)	None
0–12 percent	None	None	None
55 percent	85 percent	85 percent	55 percent (Abu Dhabi); 50 percent (Dubai).
Progressive tax structure (0–30 percent)	Progressive tax structure (0–30 percent)	Progressive tax structure (15–30 percent)	Only foreign banks are taxed on 20 percent of profits
5 percent (most products); 0 percent (food); 100 percent (alcohol and tobacco)	5 percent (most products); 0 percent (food); 100 percent (alcohol and tobacco)	5 percent (most products); 0 percent (food); 100 percent (alcohol and tobacco)	5 percent (most products); 0 percent (food); 100 percent (alcohol and tobacco)
None	None	None	None
9 percent (employer), 5 percent (employee), 2 percent (government)	None	8 percent (employer), 5 percent (employee)	12.5 percent (employer), 5 percent (employee), 2.5 percent (government)
100 RO (training tax), 2–10 percent (municipal taxes)	None	None	5 percent (hotel tax in Dubai and Abu Dhabi), 5 percent (rental tax)
Tax holidays (5 years renewable); customs duty exemptions	Tax holidays (up to 10 years); imports of raw materials not available in Qatar are duty-free	No tax holidays. Customs duty exemptions (imports of machinery and raw materials)	Tax holidays: 15 years, renewable in most free zones

1969. By 1972 oil production reached 440 million barrels and brought Abu Dhabi oil revenues worth £220,400,000.[16]

Abu Dhabi took the bulk of oil exports and with it the majority of revenues for the United Arab Emirates (see table 4.6 for UAE production figures). In 1974, Abu Dhabi accounted for 84 percent of the United Arab Emirates' total revenues. In 1976 this figure stood at 82 percent and in 1978 it was still at 77 percent (Askari, Cummings, and Glover 1982: 135). These revenues did not accrue directly to the federal state or to most of the individual emirates; rather, they went to the two most important emirates, Abu Dhabi and Dubai. While Abu Dhabi provided the majority of federal state revenues in the early years of the United Arab Emirates, this balance retreated in favor of Dubai, with Abu Dhabi still contributing more than half of the federal budget. Today the United Arab Emirates as a whole possesses the world's third largest recoverable oil reserve, with about 98 billion barrels (representing 10 percent of the world total) and a large natural gas reserve representing 4 percent of the world total. Oil production capacity stands at 3.7 million barrels a day, and actual production is about 2 million barrels a day (World Bank 2003a: 24–25).

In the United Arab Emirates the enormous oil wealth was used for the development of modern public infrastructure and the transformation of municipalities, as well as for an extensive state apparatus. Rather than investing in the military-defense complex as in Iraq, the United Arab Emirates embarked on a policy of economic development by emphasizing economic diversification. In Dubai, for example, an ambitious development policy was conducted by the regime of Sheikh Rashid bin Maktum. The development projects included urban improvement (construction of a runway in June 1965 and a bridge in May 1963), land management, and infrastructure for improved trade. Other projects included the establishment of social welfare services such as medical facilities, educational establishments, and a modern police force in 1956.

State making was characterized by the redistribution of existing oil revenues, by investment in national infrastructure, and by attempts to attract new capital investments. In this way, the United Arab Emirates combined the positive attributes of a rentier state (huge oil investment

Table 4.6. UAE oil production, 1995–2003

Year	Barrels per day (bb/d)	Value of oil exports (US$)
1995	2,200,000	—
1996	2,230,000	—
1997	2,250,000	—
1998	2,300,000	10,400,000
1999	2,070,000	14,200,000
2000	2,190,000	23,400,000
2001	2,120,000	19,733,000
2002	1,940,000	19,727,000
2003	2,260,000	25,653,000

Sources: Oil production figures for 1995–99 are from Business Monitor (2000); figures for 1999–2003 are from IMF (2004b).

and revenues) with those of a production-oriented welfare state. Its rulers followed the path of monopolizing high-value resources and exchanging them for the essential resources of rule (including oil for weapons), while at the same time pursuing the acquisition and use of new resources. The United Arab Emirates attempted to diversify its economy and to attract foreign investment as part of its plan for the post-rentier phase. Several indicators suggest that the United Arab Emirates might be moving beyond a pure rentier state. Per capita GDP in purchasing power parity has risen considerably since the late 1980s. In 1989 this stood at US$17,000 and in 2001 at US$26,000. Real GDP growth has averaged 7 percent a year since 1993. This can be attributed to rapid diversification of the non-oil sectors (energy-intensive petrochemicals, fertilizers, cement, and aluminum), and more recently tourism, re-export, trade, and manufacturing. While these non-oil sectors accounted for 70 percent of GDP and 43 percent of exports in 2000, the country's economy grew at 9 percent a year in real terms in the 1990s.

Among policies pursued during the boom years, the political leadership was committed to trade and equitable growth between the seven emirates (trade openness),[17] investments in social policies such as the Abu Dhabi Fund for Development or inter-emirate economic aid,[18] and the diversification of exports and foreign investment via free zones (creation of a favorable business climate).[19] Indeed, exports from the

United Arab Emirates relied heavily on exports from its free zones, particularly those located in Dubai; in 2002 exports stood at US$51 billion and in 2003 rose to US$61 billion.[20] In all this, the United Arab Emirates managed to use its oil revenues to develop itself as a regional hub for foreign investment in the areas of construction, tourism, waste-water treatment, desalination, natural energy exploration, and transport. While Dubai has been at the forefront of this policy, the financial crisis in 2009, the defaulting of Dubai's major investment company in late 2009 and the bailout from oil-rich Abu Dhabi might have tilted the state-making path back to a more classic rentier paradigm.

There is awareness on the part of the rulers of Dubai and Abu Dhabi of the necessity to think and act beyond the rentier state. Some of the policies point toward this, as indicated by the decision to invest in civilian nuclear energy as an alternative source of energy and in alternative infrastructure projects such as a rail system linking the different emirates. Other policies remain bound by the logic of rentierism, since the United Arab Emirates' economy remains dominated by oil and even the forward-looking projects are funded by oil revenues (thus representing simply another form of exchange of resources), and not a decision to extract them from a subject population.[21] Limits to the transformation of the rentier state are obvious, as privatization changed little in terms of the way economics and politics interact. Many of the features of a personalized economy still dominate the United Arab Emirates, such as the local sponsorship system (*kafil*), the informal nature of politics (*wasta*), and the persistence of neopatrimonial structures. Recent proposals to abolish the agency law that restricts foreigners to minority stakes are pointing toward more fundamental changes. These proposals are linked to issues of economic privilege, equal wealth distribution, and the integration of foreign workers, and hence are linked to the question of political rule and legitimacy. Economic reforms nevertheless led to a diversification of the economy based on creating new rents and a favorable investment climate. While the country has not moved completely beyond the rentier state, it finds itself in a transition period from a rentier state to a production-oriented state. This shows that rentier states will not necessarily suffer from institutional fragility and inefficiencies. Indeed, states such as the United Arab Emirates,

Bahrain, Kuwait, and Qatar have strengthened their regimes and institutions—in no small part thanks to rent revenues—and show positive side effects of state making. According to many international rankings, they have attained a high level of rule of law and governance.[22] The ostensible fragility of rentier states is thus not an inescapable natural fate of oil-exporting countries, but rather a stage in the process of state making.

Dynastic Rulers and Modern States

Ruling families provide the nucleus of political and economic life in the emirates and constitute, in terms of representation, ruling oligopolies resembling absolutist monarchs in early modern Europe (Herb 1999). Related to the question of the ruling families is the issue of citizenship and nationality. This reflects the exclusive nature of extended family rule and the preferential notion of nationality. In order to maintain state welfare in times of declining rents, the emirates have developed new rents via economic diversification, and at the same time reduced the number of those who could benefit from state welfare through the exclusion of foreign workers residing in the country. Nationality and citizenship is thus part of the rentier political bargain. Nationality may be obtained by law (*bil-qanun*), by dependence (*bil-tabi'a*) or by naturalization (*bil-tajannus*). Obtaining nationality through dependence comes via paternal lineage, while obtaining citizenship through law relates to the number of years' residence in the country, where a distinction is made between Omanis, Qataris and Bahrainis (three years), other Arabs (ten years), and all others than this (30 years) (Al-'Al 1996; Dresch 2004; Ibrahim 1978). The adoption of a citizenship law in the United Arab Emirates in 1972 was clearly driven by considerations of exclusion, security, and the maintenance of material privileges. In the amendment of 1975, certain provisions were added that allowed for citizenship to be passed on from an Emirati woman to her children. Foreign wives of Emiratis obtained citizenship which only had to be validated through an administrative process.[23] In reality, however, little changed and the practice of gaining citizenship remained complex.[24]

Nationality remains largely based on paternal lineage for the purpose of excluding certain foreign-born groups, maintaining closed communities, and privileging family structures. Citizenship is more an act of goodwill than a genuine right that can be evoked, and involves a two-class distinction between genuine Emiratis and those who, even once naturalized, pass on the status of naturalized citizen to their children (*mutajanassin*) and presumably throughout generations (Al-Rukn 2000).

As far as practice of marriage is concerned, certain self-restrictions are applied. In the case of Abu Dhabi it is reported that members of certain extended families from the Bani Yas tribe will not marry outside the family (Dresch 2004: 136–57). Reasons for this are often found in material considerations, for becoming an insider allows access to material benefits and welfare provisions, both on a micro level (the extended family) and a macro level (the nation).[25] In the realm of the latter, it is interesting to observe that the Emirate of Abu Dhabi cares first for its own citizens—via protection of property rights and gifts of various kinds, ranging from residential land to agricultural land and to a marriage grant of AED900,000 toward a house—while only secondarily supporting the larger grouping, constituting the nation, by contributing the major part of the budget of the United Arab Emirates. In 1992, for example, a marriage fund (Sunduq al-Zawaj) was established which encouraged marriage among citizens through generous payments, gifts, and loans. By the end of 1997 the marriage fund had spent an estimated AED950 million (of which AED500 million were grants) and by the end of the decade some AED1.5 billion (Dresch 2004: 148). The fund represents a massive attempt at social engineering within a state-building agenda that tries to privilege locals over foreign citizens.

* * *

Foreign workers are largely excluded from the privileged group. They represent a large percentage of the population of the United Arab Emirates. According to the 1995 census there are 600,000 Emiratis out of a total population of 2.4 million. Related to this are issues of material well-being and labor rights with respect to the foreign workforce. With 1.8 million foreign workers (representing 75 percent of the population) this issue is growing in importance, and, while in earlier years the state could afford to grant benefits to these workers, in the post-rentier era such benefits have been curbed. Many foreign migrant workers face long working hours and poor living conditions.[26] Citizenship issues in the Gulf are more than a question of identity, but rather a question about material rewards and access to resources: citizenship involves material benefits and it confers a legal status quite different from that of foreigners (Dresch 2004: 139). Fear of a demographic imbalance is prominent in the local media, with claims circulating that a third of Emirati families are "totally dependent" on south Asian domestic workers and that children will grow up speaking Tamil and not Arabic.[27] A 1995 survey showed that on average two domestic servants are employed in every national family (ibid.: 140). A campaign against illegal immigrants was mounted in 1996 to counter these popular fears. Phrases such as "Emirati society" (*al-mujtama' al-'imarati*) became commonplace and fears grew about intermarriages with foreigners and about foreign workers (ibid.: 151).[28] By 2000, officials were saying informally that the ratio of locals to foreign residents had shifted from one-third to one-fourth. Beyond the issue of citizenship, foreign residents are required to have a local sponsor (*kafil*) who owns 51 percent of an economic enterprise in order for it to engage in economic activities. This sponsor system has created a mini-system of rent distribution, in which local sponsors reap benefits for simply giving their name and signature (Beaugé 1986). Patterns of economic activity, housing, income, and social mobility depend a great deal on the distinction between locals (*muwatinin*) and migrants (*wafidin*) (Dresch 2004: 139). This distinction between locals and foreigners carries over into the realm of security. Here the primary threats to stability in the United Arab Emirates are seen to come from within. Domestic concerns include potential threats from unruly expatriates and political claims made by foreign workers. In recent years, countermeasures have been taken to curb the influence of expatriates, such as a six-month ban on re-entering the United Arab Emirates for foreigners who have cancelled their residence there.[29] Another policy measure with the same aim of curbing potential domestic threats (and the arrival of "unwanted foreigners" and relatives of expatriates) was the introduction of a salary limit for applicants seeking visas to visit.[30]

*   *   *

The United Arab Emirates embarked on a process of state making that attempts to go beyond the rentier-state bargain. In doing so, much political caution has been exercised in a bid to accommodate necessary change with the *status quo* retained as far as possible. Attempts to diversify the domestic revenue base of the state are completely avoided for fear of possible political consequences, and where limited taxation is applied this has no repercussions on the implicit domestic social contract since the costs are borne by foreign companies and foreign residents. Here, the state has managed to maintain its welfare function and commitments in both boom and bust years. The political consequences of these economic reforms have been that the linkages between declining resources and demands for political participation have been broken. No significant societal or economic pressures for political diversification exist, and consent is widely assured through material benefits.

While the United Arab Emirates did manage to cope with the fiscal challenges of the post-rentier state, the country has not fully mastered the associated social and political challenges, namely the integration of the foreign labor force. More sustained reforms aimed at diversifying the domestic revenue base of the state, for example by taxing not only foreigners but also Emiratis, are avoided for fear of political counter-demands. Sustained social reforms aimed at incorporating foreign workers into the Emirati nation are also avoided for fear of creating a larger constituency and hence a smaller share of welfare distribution for each individual within that constituency. In solving the economic problems of rentierism and in avoiding the associated political problems, the United Arab Emirates combines elements of the classical path of rentier states of predatory statehood with that of a benevolent state embedded in society. However, attempts at diversifying the economy must be accompanied by domestic resource extraction in order to produce lasting political change, fully accountable governments, and eventually a path toward democracy. None of this exists so far, as dynastic rulers in the Gulf have so far shied away from taxing their own population and rather opted for taxing foreign residents and companies. The dislocation of domestic resource extraction and democratic governance structures is a common feature of states that progress from the rentier to post-rentier path. The embrace of economic reforms without political reforms, as in the United Arab Emirates and the other Gulf states, is a clear indication of this. State making thereby sustains the rentier path of high welfare spending and autonomous political rule, without giving rise to the lack of development, market distortions, and bad governance usually associated with oil wealth. But it does not provide a pathway toward more consent and democratization.

This chapter has outlined the history of state making in the Gulf states, including a detailed study of the United Arab Emirates. It has demonstrated how abundant oil revenues gave rulers the means to exchange consent for state welfare. Oil rents served as an obstacle to the formation of democratic states, as stability has rested on a social contract that avoided bargaining over resources; but oil rents and policies of economic diversification have also allowed generous welfare spending to continue in times of fiscal hardship and thereby created embedded authority structures. Thus, while rentierism undercuts the "war-makes-states" mechanism and leads to institutionally weak states that are not based on the outcome of a ruler-subject struggle, it does allow states to provide domestic security and general welfare and compensate for absent democratic representation through socially embedded authority structures. In the absence of war making, the Gulf states have managed to transform themselves from tribal sheikhdoms into sustainable states.

5

State Failure and Peace Building

Effective rule depends on the continuous production of crucial resources. If the resources dry up, rulers lose the means of enforcing whatever decisions they make and state capacity collapses. This has happened often in history, as an anthropologist studying Central America or the Near East could readily show us.

Charles Tilly, "Grudging consent"

Patterns of state making in the Middle East stand in contrast to the European process of state making, which was primarily the outcome of the state's need to obtain financial resources for use in coercion, violence, and war making. In Europe it became politically necessary for absolutist monarchs to extend rights of representation in government to those capable of paying the taxes necessary to finance wars which states wished to fight or felt compelled to fight. This was not the case in the Middle East. Although as a region the modern Middle East has seen many interstate wars, internal wars and insurgencies, it is not war making but rather abundant oil revenues and other rents that have driven state making. Far from stabilizing the process internally, rents have led to the creation of allocation states, with bureaucracies whose primary function is to distribute revenues and to serve as employer of last resort and, contrary to the situation in Europe, not as a tool for revenue extraction or as an effective tool of state policy. Rentier states have little in common with the European experience of state making. They are characterized by weak state institutions and a malfunctioning public sector. The distinction between public and private is often blurred, and policies are implemented either in a top-down fashion or not at all. Governments have monopolized the right to extract the natural resources of the country, from which spring abundant rents, much greater than the profits which can be made in the private sector. State institutions which, since their creation, have distributed revenues cannot be expected to perform the same regulatory, extractive, and legal roles most typically ascribed to bureaucracies (Cooley 2001: 170; Schwarz 2008b). In addition, they usually do not have to tax their countries' populations and therefore have the privilege of distributing revenues without reference to economic considerations and without granting political representation to those social segments that could provide the state with capital and financial resources.

Middle Eastern Rentier States

Rentier states are those states in which revenues from rents (often oil exports) contribute well over 40 percent of the state's overall revenues. Such states stand in contrast to states that have to rely on domestic resource extraction. Rentier states enjoy a degree of autonomy from society due to the availability of abundant natural resources. They display a particular path of state making that by and large defies the European path: oil dependence created states that have low state capacity in taxation and that are autonomous from societal demands. State making has not been accompanied by political accountability, transparency, or what Charles Tilly has termed "the civilianization of government and democratization of politics" (Tilly 1990: 206). Nor has state making been accompanied by genuine democratization. The linkage between revenue and rule constitutes the raison d'être of state making and conditions the fulfillment of states' functions. The revenue of the state becomes the state.

Some scholars have raised critical positions concerning the linkage between representation and taxation and have questioned the democratizing power of taxation.[1] The evidence presented in the preceding chapters shows that one must go beyond a direct relation between taxation and democracy and rather consider the absence of taxation; this gives wealthy rentier states the privilege of disposing of their resource wealth freely and without demands for accountability. That is indeed a crucial point highlighted by early rentier state theorists in the terminology of "allocation states" (Luciani 1990). The spending effect of rentier states—namely, oil wealth being spent on patronage and thereby inhibiting latent pressures for democratization—is by far more important. The link between rentier states and democracy is thus an indirect one and the absence of rentierism (through increased taxation, for example) is not a sufficient condition for democracy, but rather a necessary condition.

*   *   *

In the Arab Middle East, state making was achieved via an implicit social contract, according to which the state used its economic resources (oil revenues, strategic rents, development aid) as a way to allow it to offer material benefits such as jobs, free education, and subsidized food to its citizens in exchange for political acquiescence. This social contract was based on an inverse logic applied to the dictum of the American Revolution, "no representation, no taxation." As long as the state did not need to tax its people (due to alternative revenues in the form of rents), demands for representation were deemed not to be legitimate. Political legitimacy was rooted in material legitimacy and the state's ability to provide welfare. Rentierism produced societal groups modeled on the state, and prevented the formation of autonomous social groups that could raise political demands. But rentierism also gave life support to weak states as it allowed state institutions and channels of patronage to continue providing general welfare and thereby to contribute to overall stability. Jordan and the United Arab Emirates as well as the other small Gulf states illustrate this. All received the greater part of their revenues from external sources—in the case of the United Arab Emirates and the Gulf states, from oil exports; in the case of Jordan, from foreign aid and workers' remittances—which allowed a generous spending policy of welfare provision to citizens.

In this way, rentierism created particular institutional structures within states. The allocation of rents follows political criteria (loyalty, proximity to rulers, family relationships) and thereby leads to a reinforcement of traditional loyalties and a lack of bureaucratic state capacity. It is not position but proximity that determines access to resources and privileges and hence the welfare of citizens. While most theories of development focus on formal institutions within countries (parliament, the judiciary, political parties, trade unions), in rentier states the bulk of transactions occur in the informal realm. In the Arab Middle East the informal nature of politics, the patrimonial nature of social interactions and the role of informal institutions are central. Social interaction and decision-making in all fields of politics are determined by highly elaborate networks of patrons and clients, by rent-seeking, by informal group structures, and by neo-patrimonialism (Ibn Khaldun 1967 [1377]; Sharabi 1988). Particularly important in this context is the notion of *wasta* ("intercession, mediation")—the social mechanism that determines allocation decisions in society, economy and politics. *Wasta* is the "lubricant of the patronage system" (Sharabi 1988: 45). Rather than labor, personal capacity, or merit, it is personal contact with political decision-makers which determines and facilitates how resources are allocated and thus how the material well-being of the individual, the family, the clan, and so on is secured. Material well-being therefore implies not only the successful pursuit of material benefits, but also non-material enhancements (jobs, positions, licenses, access to information). The result is a reversal of the genuinely capitalist relations between labor, productivity, and profit (Bellin 2002; Cunningham and Sarayrah 1993, 1994; Schlumberger 2000). *Wasta* is an economic activity which involves investments in personal relations and gains in terms of allocation of resources. Allocation networks build on existing cultural context but function via modern channels. Rent allocation preserves these but does not create them. The preservation of tradition occurs within the vicinities of modern state institutions. The use of tradition within a formally modern system creates additional transaction costs—since entrepreneurs, besides investing in personal relationships, must also invest in the formal regulation—and hinders the implementation of economic reforms. Societal norms and lack of economic development are clearly linked.

Politically, a rentier political bargain is stable only as long as sufficient resources are available to the state. Since the majority of these resources are externally accrued, rentier states can only passively redistribute them. The consolidation of states saw challenges when economic resources were no longer forthcoming, giving rise to state withdrawal from core functions and to political instabilities. This was the case in Jordan during the petrol riots in Ma'an in 1989 and the bread riots in Karak in 1996. This was also the case in Iraq at the end of the 1980–88 Iran-Iraq War. And this was the case in the United Arab Emirates and the other Gulf states during the 1990s. Jordan and the United Arab Emirates reacted with a policy of economic diversification and the acquisition of new rents, and not a policy of war making as with Iraq, and thereby created sustainable rentier structures and political stability. Taken together, rentierism produced political and social stability and acted as life support to weak and fragile states. The survival of Jordan, and the transformation of the tribal sheikhdoms in the Gulf region into sustainable states, offer clear illustrations. This cannot be explained using a "war-makes-states" logic alone; rentierism needs to be taken into account.

In fact, whether one studies the United Arab Emirates or other Gulf states such as Saudi Arabia, Kuwait, Bahrain, or Qatar, one can detect similar patterns: none of them have formed through war making and none of them relies on the state's ability to extract tax revenues from their populations. Similarly, whether one studies Jordan or comparable taxation states such as Egypt, Tunisia, or Morocco, one can observe similar patterns of regime co-optation, again not based on the effects of war making. And finally, the experience of Iraq is perhaps symptomatic for other Middle Eastern rentier states that have experienced wars and internal armed violence and that share similar patterns of public spending, such as Algeria, Libya, or Syria. The fact that Iraq failed in its project of state building and that these others didn't should not be taken as an indication that state failure is beyond the horizon.

State failure can be expected in rentier states in times of fiscal crises. As the expenditure side of public revenues is linked to a state-building agenda of creating societal peace and political acquiescence, the social contract is sustainable only as long as there are enough resources to be allocated both for the ruling elite and for the whole of society. The chances for political change increase if the state fails to fulfill its part of the social contract and thereby fails to fulfill its welfare function. In order to avoid failure, the state has to react to societal demands and broaden its legitimacy. This creates potentials for democratization or potentials for social protest.[2] In both cases temporary political instability is likely. During boom periods, political support is bought off in return for welfare benefits, while during bust periods, a renegotiating of the rentier social contract occurs. Whether a rentier state manages to initiate a stable transition to a bust period depends to a large degree on managing revenue diversification during boom years and maintaining groups attached to the state.

* * *

States in other regions of the world have experienced similar dynamics of rentierism. In Africa, state making has been driven by external revenue accumulation and the appropriation of development aid. In the absence of domestic revenue extraction, the state came to lack full empirical control over its territory and to be based on urban elites; thus, the state had to revert to war making only in order to maintain the existing political regimes and not, as in Western Europe, in order to establish full territorial control (Herbst 2000). In many cases this led to state failure and collapse. In Latin America, state making was driven by "blood and debt" and influential financial groups were less integrated into the state-society nexus and so contributed to the emergence of limited yet capable states (Centeno 2002). When war making took the form of a global war, it also had devastating consequences for states in Latin America (Rasler and Thompson 1985). In Asia, the absence of rentierism allowed for a state-formation process similar to that seen in early modern Europe; where states were faced with scarcity of natural resources (South Korea, Taiwan, Singapore), a developmental state emerged that was endowed with strong infrastructural power sufficient to push through necessary economic policies. In states where natural resources were abundant (Malaysia, Indonesia, the Philippines), state making followed a much less ambitious path and led to weak rentier structures (Doner, Ritchie, and Slater 2005) very similar to those in the Arab world. Finally, in other parts of Asia, war making has contributed to two very different experiences in state making: in Vietnam, the strengthening of the state, due to the existence of a core ethnic group that in the past served as the basis for a relatively long-standing political community, and due to the combination of war and revolution, which inspired state officials and facilitated the promulgation of a unifying national ideology; and in Afghanistan, state collapse.

Beyond Coercion, Capital and European States

The second proposition this book has advanced concerns the specific nexus between war making and state making. The proposed "war-makes-states" mechanism has not come into play in the Middle East. Although many of the region's states do spend large proportions of their revenues on defense, they escape the logic of Tilly's model of state making and show a different dynamic regarding the relationship between coercion and capital characteristic of early modern Europe. Rather than producing institutional states, militarization in the countries examined led either to a decline in institutional power (Jordan during the 1970s, Iraq during the 1980s) or to outright failure of the state (Iraq during the 1990s).

Iraq illustrates the limitations of the argument put forward by those who have advocated giving war a chance. The case of Iraq demonstrates how war making and rentierism have counterproductive effects on state making. The history of Iraq under the Baʻth regime (1968–2003) demonstrates how, given the availability of abundant financial resources, the state became centralized via violence, coercion, and a climate of fear. Here the case of Iraq was very similar to the broad trend seen in European state building. However, Iraq differed from this in that war making was applied in the interior of the country, thereby destroying not only potential political rivals and competitors to the Baʻth party, but also elements of civil society. War making therefore created major cleavages between the country's ethnic groups. Furthermore, the abundance of revenues allowed for militarization to a degree that eventually became unsustainable. This was not matched by any institutional capacity of the state. When war making was turned on exterior enemies (in the 1980–88 Iran-Iraq War and the 1990 invasion of Kuwait), the state was weakened economically and institutionally. The sanctions regime in the 1990s and the curtailing of the state meant the state was no longer in a position to provide welfare to its people. It had failed. The rentier nature of Iraq was diminished and eventually destroyed with the invasion of Iraq in 2003. The collapse of the Iraqi state in institutional terms occurred with the dismantling of state institutions in May 2003 and particularly the inability of the United States to maintain the allocation state after Saddam Hussein's regime was toppled. The reconstruction of the state post-Hussein (from 2003) has seen many of the same problems of Iraqi state making (the rentier nature of the state) and has also been marred by insecurities that make any reconstruction effort more difficult.

*   *   *

All three cases examined in the book (Iraq, Jordan, and the Gulf states) challenge Tilly's model of state making. Following the model's competition-based logic, in a non-rentier world some of these states would, at least potentially, have disappeared. Two of them (the United Arab Emirates and Jordan) would probably have been swallowed up by larger neighboring states, and one (Iraq) would have fallen apart during the twentieth century. Had it not been for the presence of rents and protection by external powers, these weak states would not have survived as independent entities. The fact that they continue to survive and are not exposed to a competition-based state system suggests that a pure logic of "war makes states" cannot explain the longevity of these states in today's world.

Thus, in theoretical terms there is a need to extend Tilly's argument regarding state making through military competition. Just as in Europe, war making has historically produced strong states, but it has also destroyed weak states that were not capable of surviving alongside stronger states (think of Venice or Savoy). Following this logic, contemporary rentier states (weak, but surviving) must be distinguished from collapsed states, where institutional order breaks down and the situation resembles that of a war of all against all. While state collapse has not been a common feature in the Arab region—in which the average tenure of a leader stood at 23 years (Kuran 1998: 112)— the history of Iraq demonstrates the destructive power of wars. This could be explained in terms of several mechanisms. One mechanism could involve the fact that war interrupts peaceful international exchange, and especially in the case of rentier states, the flow of external rents; in Iraq war resulted in international sanctions that reduced the state's revenues considerably. Another mechanism might involve the fact that rentier states such as Iraq might start wars that are relatively more destructive because such countries overestimate their military strength, in cases where tax-extracting states that are characterized by ruler—subject bargains would not. A third mechanism might involve the fact that abundant military resources might allow rentier states to fight wars even when their weak domestic economies make it difficult to stop fighting wars; Iraq's reluctance to call a halt to the war with Iran even in the face of economic difficulties hints at this. Whatever the exact mechanism might have been in the case of Iraq, there is no doubt that war contributed to the unmaking of the Iraqi state. Thus, in the contemporary developing world, war is clearly more likely to cause state failure than to make states (Taylor and Botea 2008). This effect of breaking states is sometimes mitigated by the presence of rentierism, which allows state institutions and channels of patronage to continue in operation and thereby serves as life support for potentially failed states. Where rentierism is present, as in Iraq during the 1990s, the state continues to exist, although in rudimentary form. Where rentierism is absent, as during most of Afghanistan's modern history and in Iraq after the 2003 dismantling of state institutions responsible for rent allocation (the military and the state), the state was unable to promote a common identity. The combination of rentierism and war making in the contemporary period is thus particularly deadly to states. In the Middle East, unlike Europe, wars did not make states, but destroyed them.

Taken together, the two key findings of this book offer a new reading of state making based on performance of the state, and hence present an extension of Max Weber's understanding of the state (Weber 1922). Contrary to Weber, the "natural" state does not monopolize legitimate violence, but instead brokers an elite consensus in which armed groups tolerate domestic peace in exchange for rights to extract rents. This peace is sustainable as long as enough rents are available. In that sense, and perhaps counterintuitively, failed Iraq and weak Jordan are the norm when it comes to statehood, while the United Arab Emirates and the other small Gulf states are exceptions. Indeed, the experience of Iraq, a few other states in the Middle East (Algeria, Yemen, Somalia, Libya, and Iran come to mind) and Afghanistan suggests that where states lack adequate resources for welfare, they will implode and succumb to state failure.

Practical Implications for Peace Building

The history of state making in the Middle East has enormous policy implications. Prospects for democracy and economic development look dim, given the role of state institutions in the Arab world. Ongoing attempts at economic reform have been on the whole only half-heartedly implemented. While some states have seen effective economic change, as in the case of the United Arab Emirates and other Gulf states, this has not straightforwardly led to the emergence of liberal market economies. Informal structures, patronage, and networks of *wasta* remain prominent and set the Gulf states structurally apart from liberal, competition-based market economies.[3] While displaying some elements of a modern capitalist economy (such as private ownership), the Gulf states differ in terms of contract enforcement, the assurance of property rights, and the rule of law. Key elements of market economies—competition in the economy and the self-regulating force of the market—are today absent. While competition does exist, it can be found in the *diwan* (Arabic for "room where committee meets; advisory council"), in the form of rent-seeking for the establishment of personal ties, and not in the marketplace. The economic reforms have been pursued not according to an economic logic, but according to a political logic regarding the maintenance of the status quo. Given that the very initiation of economic reforms was driven by a political logic relating to regime stability and the maintenance of political power in the hands of ruling elites, nothing less could have been expected of the continuation of these policies. In other words, economic reforms that started as genuinely political reforms could not have been expected to transform themselves into genuinely economic reforms. International policies aimed at gaining better governance ought therefore to take this structural background and the interests of incumbent elites into account when proposing economic adjustment programs. A shift from a technical understanding of governance toward a political understanding of it seems appropriate.

*   *   *

Prospects for promoting democracy are equally dim in the Arab world. Authoritarian rulers are part and parcel of Middle Eastern politics (Ayubi 1995). Few states have made effective progress toward democracy. And yet, international policies have focused in promoting democratization throughout the region. A look at the historical path of state making in early modern Europe, exemplified here by France, shows the limitations of such a policy. It becomes obvious that the pathway to the creation of the democratic state in Europe went first through authoritarian states, then through the civilianization of government and democratization of rulers (see figure 5.1). The same process might be observable in contemporary Russia and China, which have both emphasized state capacity at the expense of democracy (Tilly 2007a). Why would that process be different in the Arab world?

While current policies of democracy promotion imply an inverse path (from democratic governance to state strength), there are reasons to doubt the feasibility of this on a theoretical level. More particularly with regard to the Middle East, an additional element needs to be taken into consideration: namely, the informal nature of politics (based on the notions of patronage networks, neo-patriarchy, and neo-patrimonialism), in order to gear policies of democracy promotion designed for formal institutions (such as parliaments or non-governmental organizations) to their desired outcome in a context of informal institutions.

This book has demonstrated that the foundation of contemporary authoritarian Arab states must first be understood before prospects for democracy in the region can be advanced. Possibilities for external actors in pushing for political reform are limited in view of the autonomy of the state, the linkages between social groups and the state (resulting in vested interests against reform), and the informal nature of politics. Possibilities for external actors seem to be best in times of sustained fiscal crisis (Waterbury 1998: 163). In this case, the international financial institutions and Western donor countries receive increased importance for rentier states as potential donors or rent providers. Political rhetoric

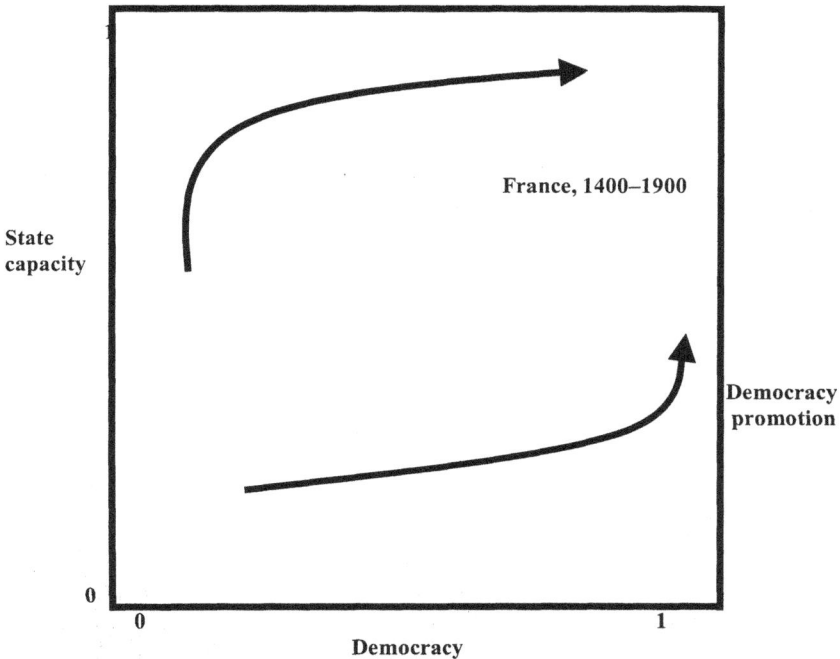

Figure 5.1. The rise of the modern state and current democracy promotion strategies (source: Tilly 2007b).

becomes important as a reference for political action, because the state is pursuing a strategy of adaptation—that is, political liberalization as a survival strategy—which will allow it to receive the best conditions for an international loan or debt rescheduling. If an internal strategy of better revenue use is employed, economic reforms are pursued, often only very partially, however, in order to balance with political considerations of regime survival. In both cases, the process is driven by local elites and external actors can only advise and sustain the chosen path.

*　　*　　*

The relevance to policy of an analytical refinement of existing theories regarding state making becomes even more accentuated in light of recent interventionist policies in world politics, and particular in view of recent attempts to rebuild the state in Iraq. The relevance of understanding state making in its theoretical and practical scope is most evident in the area of post-conflict peace building. Here, the tension has been one of rebuilding war-torn societies through the imposition of international administrations. This has involved a merging of peacekeeping with state-building agendas (United Nations and Boutros-Ghali 1992; United Nations and Brahimi 2000). Peace building in its current form is hence distinct from peacekeeping in its classical sense, since the former entails elements of state reconstruction and the imposition of state functions on societies, as witnessed in East Timor, Kosovo, Iraq, and Afghanistan (Caplan 2005; Chesterman 2004). These ambitious international efforts and the complex nature of post-conflict situations demand knowledge of several interrelated processes, most notably the historical process of state making and state-society relations.

The tensions within these projects can be exemplified with regard to the three core functions of statehood (security, welfare, representation). International efforts in state building have in recent years focused on building liberal, reformed states (leaner government), and not strong, effective welfare states (larger states). However, this international reform agenda, most evident in the Washington consensus, implies an insuperable tension between objectives (Fukuyama 2004; Milliken and Krause 2002; Schwarz 2005). This tension involves both security-related and economic matters. A global liberal economic order demands strong states, since weak and corrupt states do not attract foreign investments or international companies; for such reasons these states have been referred to as the "black holes" of the world economy (Wolf 2004). In security terms, the lack of state capacity has come to impact on the developed world directly, as illustrated by the attacks of 9/11, and weak states have become a problem of the international political order. The logical conclusion seems to be that this renewed preoccupation with weak states will shift the focus of international peace-building efforts onto creating effective state structures rather than democratic polities.

The need for strong states is relevant not only for the state-building agenda in the developing world, but also for debates on the reform of strong state institutions in Western Europe. While in recent years many calls have been made to render strong states more competitive (especially in the realm of taxation) and to make democratic governments leaner, such an approach endangers the very foundations of the modern state as a provider of public goods irrespective of the addressee. The fulcrum of the modern state remains its constitutional basis—the notion of a civil or social contract between rulers and ruled—and its preservation of individual freedoms. A change from a constitutional state to a performance-oriented lean state (based on concepts of citizens paying for public services such as rule of law and education) would have profound implications for the foundations of modern states.

* * *

State failure is another policy area for which an understanding of state making has enormous implications. Although for centuries armed violence was the driving force in building viable states on the European continent, recent years have witnessed more and more occurrences of state failure precisely due to such conflict. While this phenomenon has mistakenly been seen by many as the unmaking of the international order, the state system has actually allowed for the disappearance of states in only a few cases. Historical studies show that state disappearance has been rare in world history. Between 1415 and 1987 there are only 11 cases of an entity shifting from sovereign to dependent status and 15 cases where states merged or were dissolved (Strang 1991). This book has highlighted the important difference between institutional state collapse and functional state failure. It has argued that an understanding of potential state failure (when and where will it occur? Under what circumstances do states fail?) and policies of addressing this through prevention and peace building (how can failed states be rebuilt? What is the role of the international community in all of this?) have to start with an understanding of the basic functions of the modern state. These three core functions (security, welfare, and representation) do not exist in a vacuum and are closely interconnected. In some cases they reinforce each other and in others they hinder each others' fulfillment (Schwarz 2005).

Understanding the potential for state failure must start with an understanding of how these three functions interact in a given state. The empirical chapters of this book have shown that rentier states display a particular connection between these functions: abundant external revenues allow the provision of welfare and the acquisition of security, to the detriment of representation. In times of fiscal crisis the state has to withdraw its welfare function and re-negotiate a new equilibrium. This can involve taking on an external strategy (revenue acquisition and/or war making) or an internal strategy (economic reform and/or democratization). Both scenarios bring the danger of state failure, as war making may lead to the unmaking of the state and economic reform may increase societal conflict. In both cases the heritage of a rentier economy, and the informal nature of revenue distribution within a rentier state, brings the potential for state failure.

A failed state can be defined as "a polity that is no longer able or willing to perform the fundamental tasks of a nation-state in the modern world" despite maintaining international legal recognition (Rotberg 2004: 6). A failed state is thus not the same as a collapsed state. State collapse involves the breakdown of state institutions and the emergence of a situation that resembles a war of all against all. Its symptoms are anarchy and widespread violence that threaten surrounding states and regions.[4] State failure, on the other hand, typically precedes but does not always lead to state collapse and should be understood more broadly.

Thus, politically speaking, state failure is the failure of good governance, in the security field the failure to provide protection and stability equally to all citizens in a non-discriminatory way, and in the economic domain the failure to provide welfare—the latter being the most important in the long term. Therefore, fragile states are states that have weak structures and lack performance capacity in core state tasks; they may be on the verge of becoming failed states, but may also recover from state weakness and gain in capacity to perform. State failure where it has occurred has essentially involved a collapse of the patronage system which previously maintained a minimum level of order and a selective form of economic welfare (for those clients of the rulers). Even where internationally mandated economic reforms have reduced the economic resources available to shadow states, finances are often channeled through other means, such as non-state organizations

(Pouligny 2005). Comparing the collapse of rentier states, one observes the importance of maintaining the distribution of welfare benefits (even at a low level) to allow the continuing operation of the security function of the state. Where both collapse, as in post-2003 Iraq, insecurities and the imposition of the monopoly on the legitimate use of violence (the first step in state building) becomes the highest priority. The prime considerations for rentier states are thus budget security (Brand 2001), the acquisition of new rents, and the maintenance of the state's allocation power in the face of weak infrastructural power. Thus, gradual reform of post-rentier states is the key to transforming an allocation state into a taxation state, and to transforming weak states into legitimate democratic states. That effective central control of the state is a prerequisite for this has been argued above. From this perspective, the future of the non-rentier states seems perhaps brighter than that of rentier states such as Iraq or Saudi Arabia.

*   *   *

Finally, the analysis of state-making processes in the Middle East offers some theoretical conclusions. It questions standard assumptions about the emergence of the nation-state (Migdal 2004; Leander 2004). A refinement of Tilly's approach to state making therefore ought to include a critical awareness of different historical contexts (the early modern era in contrast to today's globalized world) and different geographical contexts (the cultural background of the Arab Middle East, against which modern state building occurs). While it is true that predatory states are today marginal in world geography, examples do still exist. Many of these modern predatory states are situated precisely in the Arab Middle East and thus warn against dropping Tilly's approach to state making completely. The usefulness of Tilly's account lies exactly in the fact that it highlights the importance for state making of institutions of organized violence. While only detailed empirical analyses can show to what degree war making and militarization influence state making, Tilly's approach should not be discarded from the outset.

This book ultimately underlines the importance of analyzing the revenue structure of the state. While in early modern Europe war making was the main function and goal for which revenues were levied, these functions and goals will vary over time. Today's states compete primarily in terms of economic growth and economic development, and less so in terms of militarily might and war making. Revenues have remained important. Without them, states cannot fulfill their functions. With them, the prosperity and improvement of nations increase, as Edmund Burke remarked:

> The revenue of the state is the state. In effect all depends upon it, whether for support or for reformation . . . Through the revenue alone the body politic can act in its true genius and character and therefore it will display just as much of its collective virtue, and as much of that virtue which may characterize those who move it, and are, as it were, its life and guiding principle, as it is possessed of a just revenue . . . The prosperity and improvement of nations has generally increased with the increase of their revenues; and they will both continue to grow and flourish, as long as the balance between what is left to strengthen the efforts of the individuals, and what is collected for the common efforts of the state, bear to each other a due reciprocal proportion, and are kept in a close correspondence and communication. (Burke 1790: 334–35)

The framework of state making which this book has outlined offers a way to explain this. It suggests one way of interpreting state making with a focus on the fragility of most Middle Eastern states. The limited institutionalization as well as the limited political legitimacy of all but a few states stand out as significant characteristics. Today the Middle East, even more than in other parts of the world, finds itself confronted by many challenges in the fields of security, welfare, and representation. These challenges are increased by pressures posed by globalization—pressures that require responses from governments all over the world. But the Arab world has resisted these pressures in terms of peace building, economic reform, and democratization, and effective governance remains a strategic challenge to all states of the region.

Epilogue

Arab states are often seen as exceptional and anomalous creatures within a turbulent and hostile world. And recent developments at the beginning of 2011 in Tunisia, Egypt, and Libya seem to support this view.

However, these developments have nothing anomalous about them. They must be understood in view of the unfinished state-building processes these states have undergone since their independence. These states all had repressive political power but lacked the tools of state power, namely taxation, embedded political authority, and most importantly, popular legitimacy. They were all in search of legitimacy and good governance.

Revolutions and regime changes were almost annual occurrences in the 1950s and 1960s in the Arab world. Since then few changes have taken place and the average tenure of an Arab leader stood until recently at twenty-three years. Hosni Mubarak came to power in 1981, Ben Ali assumed leadership of Tunisia in 1987, and Muammar Qaddafi has ruled Libya since 1969.

Why Now These Revolts and Not Earlier?

The recent wave of protests in the Arab world has its origin in unfulfilled socio-economic demands. For decades, Arab rulers maintained a social contract by which political and human rights were traded for social and economic opportunities. Political dissidence was not allowed to be voiced as long as individuals had job opportunities and society enjoyed broad-based welfare. This system functioned as long as enough revenues were available to be distributed to loyal groups around rulers and society at large. Years of mismanagement, delayed economic reform, and most recently the effects of the world financial crisis have put great strains on this system. Food and bread prices had to be raised and gasoline prices rocketed, all this in a context where social welfare was the test for a regime's legitimacy. The protests in Tunisia and Egypt were initially inspired by the increase in food and bread prices and by the lack of welfare provisions by the government; only then did the protests turn into political demands. The lack of receptiveness of the government to these demands has led to a radicalization of the demands, with the known results of the resignation of the presidents of Tunisia and Egypt.

What Are Expectations for the Future of the Middle East, and Who Is Next?

The events in Tunisia and Egypt and the change of power have given rise to expectations that similar developments could occur elsewhere. States that have long delayed reforms are hence more likely to see protests, and the wave of contention that hit Libya in February 2011 indicates this. Nevertheless, governments are not prone to fail so rapidly, as the rebellion in Libya shows. Regimes may avoid failure by engaging in genuine political reform, with the aim of changing the structure of governance and government. And they may engage in genuine economic and financial reforms to bring about development. If they manage to generate new revenues for welfare, they will survive. If they lack adequate resources for welfare, they will fall apart from inside and succumb to their fragility.

What Can the West Do?

The West—Europe and the United States—has a priori no role in the current wave of contestation in the Arab world. These are domestic issues and are not linked to the broader geo-political context. In concrete terms, the West can do very little once protests and revolts break out. It can only call for the respect of human rights and the right of peaceful protest. The whole debate about a humanitarian intervention in Libya and the establishment of a "no-fly-zone" has pointed the wrong way, as it has seen military action and war making as a tool of state building. None of this can effectively be implemented if interventions and military actions—no matter how well intended—are misperceived and lack popular legitimacy. Using war making to rescue states and build them anew is not a sustainable option for the West, as is evident from the recent history of Iraq. And Libya is no exception to this. State building requires more than military tools; it demands a genuinely comprehensive approach toward building security, welfare, and representation in a country. However, the West can play an important role in contributing toward long-term stability in the region. It must start thinking about how states can be supported *before* they fail. How can genuine political and economic reform be enacted while stability still reins? It is common sense to know that state building is a long and arduous process driven by domestic actors; this process passes first through the creation of an effective and strong state and only secondly moves into democratization. What the Arab world is currently witnessing are demands for that second process of democratization to take roots. The West must recognize that it cannot influence that process. However, it must monitor closely how governments in those states not yet touched by popular protest have dealt with the challenges of decreasing welfare, economic decline, and decreasing societal well-being. From such analyses it can then deduce and anticipate where and when state failure most likely will occur.

Notes

Introduction

1. The term "Arab Middle East" is used here in a political rather than geographical sense. It includes not only the Middle East proper (Egypt, Jordan, Lebanon, Syria, Iraq, Kuwait, Bahrain, Qatar, Saudi Arabia, the United Arab Emirates, Oman, Yemen), but also the North African states of Morocco, Tunisia, Algeria, and Libya. The total number of states in the Arab world thus includes 16 sovereign states plus the special case of Palestine. Non-Arab Middle Eastern states such as Israel, Turkey and Iran are excluded.

2. The term "rentierism" refers to the (relative) dependence of states on rents for their internal functioning. Rents are understood to be forms of income generated from the export of natural resources, usually oil and gas, but also income from bilateral or multilateral foreign aid payments, such as development or military assistance. Rentier states are those states in which revenues from rents contribute well over 40 percent of the state's overall revenue.

3. There are historical examples where the territory held by states has changed. In 1990 the two Yemeni states united; another case in point is the example of the short-lived United Arab Republic (1958–61). There are also cases of states that have never actually formed despite attempts to make this happen: for example, so far there is no independent Kurdish state, independent Christian state in Lebanon, or independent Palestine.

4. This view focuses on a state's purpose and its fulfillment of basic human needs. It also allows for a minimization of the role of the state and the role of non-state actors in the fulfillment of these basic needs.

5. In September 1970, Syrian troops entered Jordanian territory; they advanced as far as the northern city of Irbid before eventually withdrawing (Razoux 1999: 20–21). Two Jordanian armored brigades (the 40th and 60th) participated in the 1973 Yom Kippur War, as did three artillery units in support

of Syria. Ironically, the same Jordanian 40th Armored Brigade had rebuffed the Syrian army as it crossed into Jordan in 1970; at that time the brigade destroyed more than 100 Syrian vehicles. In the 1973 war Jordanian support for the Syrian army came without great enthusiasm; King Hussein had reluctantly agreed to join the Arab war effort against Israel by dispatching, on 14 October, the elite 40th Armored Brigade under the command of Brigadier-General Habis Al-Majali and then, on 23 October, the 60th Armored Brigade (ibid.: 134–43).

Chapter 1. Understanding State Making

1. I have first elaborated this tripartite framework of analysis in Schwarz 2005 and further developed it in Schwarz 2010. The following sections draw on these elaborations.

2. A critical discussion of this can be found in Migdal (2001: 13–15). The criticism raised here and throughout the book does not relate to Weber's own work, in which notably the aspect of legitimacy has paramount importance, but rather to neo-Weberian scholarship which ignores this aspect.

3. On the different paths European state building took in the early modern period, see Downing (1992) and Strayer (1970).

4. A more cautious note is provided by Hood (2003: 232), who asserts that "there are no strong reasons for expecting the tax state to face a sudden major loss of overall taxable capacity." The information age offers at the same time more possibilities for non-state actors to escape taxation (ibid.: 227).

5. A general personal income tax has been in existence in both Morocco and Tunisia since 1989. In Morocco it was installed via law number 17–89 of 21 November 1989 (as published in the *Official Gazette* of 6 December 1989) and in Tunisia through law number 89–114 of 30 December 1989 (as published in the *Official Gazette* of 31 December 1989). Both countries also have a general company tax—Morocco's dates from 1986 and Tunisia's from 1989 (Butzclaar-Mohr 1992).

6. All subsequent figures are the author's own calculations for the years 1999 to 2004, based on data from the Economist Intelligence Unit (various years; various countries).

7. This is the average for 1993–96 (Springborg and Henry 2001: 77).

8. The low level of taxation in oil-rentier states might actually indicate that the state does not have to tax its people. Hence the need for taxation is low, but the state's capacity to tax is not necessarily also low (this might incidentally be the case also). A more obvious case is that of states that rely on both taxation and rents, but which use indirect means to raise revenues. Here the state clearly lacks capacity, for it has to revert to indirect measures.

9. Following the indicators given above, both Syria and Yemen can properly be called rentier states as rents contribute more than 40 percent of state revenues (see also Table 1.3).

10. The Paris Protocol of April 1994 (extended under the September 1995 Interim Agreement) gave the Palestinian Authority (PA) the right to set its own tariffs and to levy taxes. The protocol stipulates that value-added tax is to be based on the Israeli system and placed at 15–16 percent (lower than the 17 percent in Israel). However, the figures assembled here are misleading with regard to the nascent Palestinian's state infrastructural power, since the state of Israel in fact collects income tax for the PA from Palestinian workers in Israel. Israel can keep 25 percent of these earnings, but has to forward the rest to the PA. The income from this clearance revenue system is the most important source of finance for the PA besides foreign grants. Estimates place it at more than 60 percent of total revenues.

11. As historians of taxation have shown, "the true magnitude and significance of the tax load have in the past been concealed from the people. The fiscal principle would have to yield to the economic principle; the direct method of raising state revenues should become the rule and the indirect method the exception" (Wicksell 1988: 128).

Chapter 2. Iraq: From Rentier State to Failed State

1. Some observers have argued that in 2003 there was little Iraq could have done to prevent its invasion and destruction at the hands of outside forces, and that the decision for such actions was taken elsewhere. Hence they prefer to refer to Iraq as a destroyed rather than a failed state (Metz 2010: 55). I agree with these observations, but in this chapter wish to underline the point that before the 2003 invasion Iraq had already failed as a state. The reference to Iraq as a "failed state" makes no judgment on the legitimacy of the invasion but highlights the point that state making came to a (temporary) halt in 2003 and that there has been an arduous process of state reconstruction thereafter.

2. Even the elections for the Constituent Assembly in 1922 to 1924 were marred by rumors of vote-rigging (Al-Adhami 1979: 26). The high hopes attached to the elections in 1936 and 1937 were equally short-lived, as the electoral experience was abandoned and repression won over (Hadhri 1978: 211–14).

3. It is interesting, and of course brutally sad, that the outside world did not step in to bring about a ceasefire between Iran and Iraq. That the international community did intervene when Iraq engaged in war making again in 1990–91 is even more cynical and shows the operation of great-power politics in the international relations of the Middle East at its most extreme.

4. In 1927 exploration rights were granted to the Iraqi Petroleum Company (IPC), which despite its name was British. Questions of nationalization came to the fore after the revolution of July 1958; the government seized 99 percent of IPC in December 1961 and in 1973 fully nationalized the company.

5. In the mid-1970s, personal income up to an annual level of 500 dinars was theoretically subject to a 5 percent tax, with tax gradually increasing for income of 500–1,000 dinars to 10 percent. The tax drastically increased for the richest in society, where income above 15,000 dinars was taxed at 75 percent (Askari, Cummings, and Glover 1982: 108).

6. In the 1960s an individual had to earn nearly seven times the per-capita income (based on the year 1963) before being subject to a personal income tax. For a married man with dependents under the age of 18, earnings would have to exceed 14 times the per-capita income before tax assessment would occur. Furthermore, about 91 percent of all personal income tax paid came from residents of the province of Baghdad. The concentration of income taxpayers was so extreme that in 1966 less than 1 percent of the entire population paid any income tax (Sharif 1968: 543–55).

7. These benefits allocated to society came mainly in the form of state-provided jobs. At the end of 1991 the civilian branch of the state employed 21 percent of the working population and 40 percent of Iraqi households depended directly on government payments (Dodge 2003: 160).

8. The passage from the UN mission's report can be found at S/22366, paragraph 37; for the two resolutions see UNSCR 687 (1991) and UNSCR 986 (1995). The oil-for-food program was terminated on 31 May 2004.

9. Estimates are for the summer of 1991, as mentioned in the report of the UN mission headed by Sadruddin Aga Khan (S/22799 of 17 July 1991).

10. Some observers, including former chief weapons inspector Hans Blix, have argued that the situation today would have been better had the 2003 war not taken place. Again this is a moot point, as state making clearly came to a halt in 2003 and the situation has since been characterized as one of state reconstruction.

11. Part of the reasons for the difficult process of post conflict reconstruction in Iraq can be found in the incoherent planning of the United States for the aftermath of the invasion (Ricks 2006) and the opposing views between civilians in the administration and military leaders (West 2009). One of the key points of contention was what (if any) role the "old" Iraqi army should have in post-conflict reconstruction. The decisions by the Coalition Provisional Authority (CPA) to disband the Iraqi army (by CPA order no. 2) and the order for De-Ba'thification (by CPA order no. 1) had devastating consequences in

terms of security and welfare; in the former case it deprived some 300,000 officers of their regular income and in the latter it disenfranchised some 30,000 former government officials of taking any role in reconstructing Iraq (Gordon and Trainor 2006).

12. Gen. Lance L. Smith, U.S. Air Force, NATO's former Supreme Allied Commander Transformation, in an interview with Agence France-Presse on 3 October 2006.

13. Recently affirmed by former U.S. ambassador to Iraq Ryan Crocker, in an article entitled "Dreams of Babylon," published on 22 June 2010 (Crocker 2010). This is noteworthy as Crocker is not known for pessimism as to the future of Iraq, as became evident from his testimony before the U.S. Congress in September 2007.

14. *BBC*, 2 February 2007, based on a U.S. National Intelligence Estimate. http://news.bbc.co.uk/2/hi/middle_east/6324767.stm

15. *Reuters*, 3 August 2006, based on a leaked diplomatic telegram. http://news.bbc.co.uk/2/hi/uk_news/5240808.stm

16. *New York Times*, 3 August 2006. http://www.nytimes.com/2006/08/04/world/middleeast/04rumsfeld.html

17. *International Herald Tribune*, 10 July 2006. http://www.nytimes.com/2006/07/09/world/africa/09iht-iraq.2154437.html

18. United States 2005.

19. Figures are from the Economist Intelligence Unit (various years). The figures for February 2004 are from Economist Intelligence Unit (2004a: 33).

20. *Wall Street Journal*, 9 August 2010. http://online.wsj.com/article/SB10001424052748703748904575411231275371108.html

21. In the document presented to the UN, the Kurds claim that (Southern) Kurdistan was recognized under the Treaty of Sevres (N.B. section 3, articles 62 and 64) and that the region was illegally annexed by Iraq in December 1925. They reclaim the right of self-determination according to GA Res. 1514 (XV) and underline their demands with 1,732,535 collected signatures (Memorandum from the Delegation of the Referendum Movement, dated 5 January 2005).

22. Article 110(1) of the constitution reads: "The federal government will administer oil and gas extracted from current fields in cooperation with the governments of the producing regions and provinces on condition that the revenues will be distributed fairly in a manner compatible with the demographical distribution all over the country. A quota should be defined for a specified time for affected regions that were deprived in an unfair way by the former regime or later on, in a way to ensure balanced development in different parts of the country. This should be regulated by law."

Chapter 3. Jordan: Rentierism and State Survival

1. See Introduction, note 5.

2. Some authors speak of Glubb's "humane imperialism" (Bocco and Tell 1994: 120–27); others mention his personal efforts, leadership, and diplomatic skills (El-Edroos 1980).

3. Besides a ministry for agriculture, for example, a ministry for water and irrigation has been in existence since 1988. Further state agencies exist, such as the Jordan Valley Authority and the Water Authority of Jordan.

4. Hafez al-Assad, president of Syria from 1971 to 2000, was at that time Minister of Defense and commander-in-chief of the air force. He opposed the Syrian intervention in Jordan from the beginning, and his refusal to deploy the Syrian air force obliged his rivals in the Syrian regime to abandon the intervention into Jordan and withdraw the troops (L. C. Brown 1984: 209).

5. The cases of 'Adnan 'Abu 'Odeh (Chief of the Royal Court) and Raja'i Dajani (Minister of Interior) provide examples of Palestinians who rose to prominent positions in the government under King Hussein.

6. The Palestinian population was better able to cope with these changes due to its established dominance in the private sector. The promotion of cheap labor in the qualified industrial sector was initially meant to provide welfare to Bedouin and East Bank families, but has generated welfare in urban areas instead.

7. After 2002 the United States launched a campaign of free-trade negotiations (under the Trade Promotion Authority), thereby increasing the number of countries that have signed a bilateral agreement with the United States. In the Middle East this includes Israel (1985), Jordan (2000), Bahrain (2004), Morocco (2006) and Oman (2006). In 2005 the United States also began free-trade negotiations with the United Arab Emirates and in 2006 with Kuwait and Qatar.

Chapter 4. The Gulf States: From Tribal Sheikhdoms to Sustainable States

1. Kuwait, for its part, was invaded in 1990 by Iraq and its infrastructure largely destroyed. However, Kuwait was not a war-making state but rather subject to the devastating consequences of war. While the country suffered high costs from war, it did not employ war making as a state making strategy either before or after the invasion.

2. The United Arab Emirates spent only about 5 percent of its GDP on defense-related issues during much of the late 1980s and the 1990s, and in recent years (since 2003) has spent only around 3 percent of GDP on this. Saudi Arabia and Oman, two regional neighbors that are themselves rentier

states, have each spent about 15 percent of GDP during the same period; Saudi Arabia peaks in some years at just above 30 percent of GDP, so is properly classified as a state with a high degree of war-preparedness (author's calculations based on IISS, various years).

3. The six emirates were Abu Dhabi, Dubai, Sharjah, 'Ajman, 'Umm al-Quwain, Ra's al-Khaimah and Fujairah. In 1972 Ra's al-Khaimah joined the union as its seventh member. Initial negotiations prior to the establishment of the United Arab Emirates had also included proposals to include Bahrain and Qatar in the union, but these ultimately remained independent states.

4. Identical agreements were concluded with Oman, Bahrain and Kuwait, and also with the states on the southwestern coast of the Arabian Peninsula, and along the northwestern frontier of India.

5. An extreme example of these conflicting allegiances was the case of 'Abdullah bin Khamis, who was the ruler of Daqta within the territory of Ra's al-Khaimah, but was also from the Naqbi tribe and hence a subject of the Qasimi Sheikh. After Khamis was killed in 1928 by members of the Sharqi tribe (subjects of the ruler of Fujairah), resolution of the dispute involved three sovereign rulers (see India Office Records R/15/1/278, as cited in Heard-Bey 1996: 443).

6. Given the changing loyalties, it is not enough simply to enumerate the tribes under a given ruler's authority, as allegiance would vary over time (in the case of the Na'im tribe even at times extending to the Sultan of Oman), and tribes were never permanent subjects.

7. Examples are the wars of Sheikh Zayed bin Khalifa in 1887 and 1891. In 1905, a general peace was agreed.

8. The agreements by the two sides to hand over the issue to international arbitration can be found, in full, in Kelly (1964). It is interesting to note that the Saudi government had already brought forward proposals for the delineation of the southern and eastern frontier of Saudi Arabia in 1935; in these they claimed territory only up to a point 150 miles west of Buraimi. It seems that rumors about the presence of oil in the area had changed the givens by the early 1950s (Kelly 1956: 324).

9. The Trucial Oman Scouts were established in 1951 as the Trucial Oman Levies. They operated under a British commander and reported to the British political agent in the Persian Gulf. In 1955 the unit numbered around 500 men. By the time of the United Arab Emirates' creation in 1971 the unit had become a mobile force of some 1,600 men, led by some 30 British officers assisted by Jordanian noncommissioned officers.

10. There have recently been signs of accommodation (*Khaleej Times*, 20 June 2005; *Gulf News*, 20 June 2005).

11. The fact that borders were imposed by the United Kingdom does not automatically imply that this occurred in an arbitrary or haphazard manner. British policy in this regard was driven by the perception that an expansionist Saudi Arabia was surrounded by less powerful states, so British policy attempted to address this perceived imbalance (Schofield and Blake 1988: v–xvii).

12. One example is the dispute between Sharjah and Fujairah at Dibba that resulted in fighting in the summer of 1972 (Walker 1994).

13. The unresolved territorial dispute with Iran concerns the islands of Abu Musa (Jazirah ' Abu Musa) and Tunb (Tunb as-Sughra and Tunb al-Kubra) in the Gulf. For a detailed analysis, see Mobley (2004).

14. Sexton (1994: 14–20). It is also worth noting that under the law, as promulgated by Decree Law No. 9 of 1989, citizens from countries of the Gulf Cooperation Council (GCC) are treated as Qatari nationals.

15. Bahrain had been the regional front-runner in this category. In 1932, oil was discovered in Bahrain and after the signing of an agreement for oil exploration, production commenced quickly.

16. Figures are based on data from the Central Bank. http://www.central bank.ae/en/index.php

17. Each emirate has tried to foster its own comparative advantages in trade, with Abu Dhabi focusing on energy-based industries; Dubai on commerce, telecommunications, tourism, and financial services; Sharjah on textiles and light manufacturing; and the northern emirates on agriculture, cement, and shipping. Another indicator of trade openness is that effective trade tariffs stand at 4 percent.

18. Rizvi (1993: 667) provides a good overview of policies aimed at accommodating to the needs of the poorer northern emirates.

19. Another attempt has involved trying to lessen the United Arab Emirates' reliance on the U.S. dollar by diversifying foreign reserves with euros (98 percent of the United Arab Emirates' foreign reserves are still in U.S. dollars). In 2005, the governor of the central bank, Sultan bin Nasser al-Suwaidi, announced that up to 5 percent of the US$19.1 billion would be transformed into euros. This reliance is linked in general terms to the rentier nature of the economy, since the United Arab Emirates—like most countries in the Middle East—has pegged its currency to the U.S. dollar in order to facilitate comparability with the world oil price (also in U.S. dollars). Due to the devaluation of the dollar in recent years (since January 2001 by some 35 percent toward the euro), some voices within OPEC have raised the possibility of selling oil on

the world market in euros, as was parenthetically announced by Iraq prior to the U.S.-led invasion of 2003.

20. *Middle East Monitor*, October 2004.

21. *Emirates Bulletin*, 19 October 2004.

22. Barro (2000); see also the *Freedom House Index* (various years) and the *Polity IV Index* (various years). However, problems remain with regard to good governance as opposed to effective governance (see World Bank 2003b; United Nations Development Programme 2004).

23. In 1999, the head of the Naturalization and Residency Prosecution spoke as if the 1972 law still applied (Dresch 2004: 266).

24. Attempts at passing a new law on citizenship that does away with some of the existing ambiguities have made no significant progress and have now virtually come to a stop. In April 2006 the Labor Ministry announced that a law was in the making pertaining to the rights of workers to form trade unions and bargain collectively. The announcement came after a week when 2,500 laborers rioted at a Dubai construction site and Human Rights Watch published a report outlining the dire situation of foreign workers in Dubai (*New York Times*, 1 April 2006; *Gulf News*, 2 April 2006; Human Rights Watch 2006).

25. It must be added, however, that the issue is more one of access (the Arabic term *wasta* again denoting the possibility of mediation) than direct blood descent.

26. As reported in Dutta (2005), journalists have documented cases in which Indian workers were promised a monthly salary of AED900 (roughly US$245); a 48-hour working week with overtime, complimentary accommodation, food, and medical insurance; a return air ticket at the end of the three-year contract; and 30 days' paid leave a year. However, upon arrival in the United Arab Emirates they had their passports confiscated by their local (Emirati) sponsors and received a monthly salary of only AED700 (US$204).

27. *Gulf News*, 2 November 2006.

28. In the United Arab Emirates no official law has yet been passed, although a draft is supposedly in the making (*Al-Ittihad*, 24 April 1999). Several decrees also exist: an unpublished presidential decree (of 19 December 1996) forbade women to marry foreigners or give up their citizenship; a second unpublished decree, dated 25 January 1997, clarified the point that the definition of foreigner did not include GCC citizens. In Qatar, where similar concerns abound, a law was even passed in 1989 (Law No. 21) that banned marriage of certain state employees to foreigners.

29. The six-month ban is imposed on all expatriates who cancel their residency and leave the country, with only a few exceptions granted. Further restrictions include a probationary period for household aid workers, who will

have to bear the cost of repatriation in case the contract is cancelled during that period (*Gulf News*, 4 January 2005).

30. *Gulf News*, 4 January 2005. Personal testimonies abound regarding the arbitrary application of new rules.

Chapter 5. State Failure and Peace Building

1. Notably Herb 2003.

2. Thus, while rentier states serve as a strong impediment for democratic rule (M. Moore 2004; Ross 2001), the presence of a fiscal crisis can raise expectations that a country may embark on a process of democratization without however guaranteeing the outcome (Luciani 1994).

3. Schlumberger (2008) has captured the newly emerging structures in the notion of patrimonial capitalism.

4. Zartman (1995), Goldstone et al. (2000), and Helman and Ratner (1992–93) all focus narrowly on "widespread violence" in failed states, and not as I do on performance and governance.

Bibliography

Official Reports and Publications

Amnesty International. 2002. *Jordan: Security Measures Violate Human Rights.* London: Amnesty International. http://www.amnesty.org/en/library/info/ MDE16/001/2002

———. 2005. *Tunisia: Human Rights Abuses in the Run-Up to the WSIS.* London: Amnesty International. http://www.amnesty.org/en/library/info/ MDE30/019/2005

Bahrain. 2006. *Mizania ad-dauliyya li-l 'am 2005–2006* (*State Budget for the Fiscal Years 2005 and 2006*). Manama: Ministry of Finance, Bahrain.

Business Monitor. 2000. *Quarterly Forecast Report: Q4 2000.* London. Business Monitor International.

Central Bank of Jordan. 1999. *Thirty Fifth Annual Report, 1998.* Amman: Department of Research and Studies.

Economist Intelligence Unit. 1996a. *Jordan: Country Profile 1996–97.* London: Economist Publications.

———. 1996b. *Tunisia: Country Profile 1996–97.* London: Economist Publications.

———. 1996c. *Algeria: Country Profile 1996–97.* London: Economist Publications.

———. 1996d. *Syria: Country Profile 1996–97.* London: Economist Publications.

———. 1997. *Tunisia: Country Profile 1997–98.* London: Economist Publications.

———. 1998a. *Algeria: Country Profile 1997–98.* London: Economist Publications.

———. 1998b. *Yemen: Country Profile 1997–98.* London: Economist Publications.

———. 1998c. *Tunisia: Country Profile 1997–98.* London: Economist Publications.

———. 1999a. *Jordan: Country Profile 1999–2000.* London: Economist Publications.

———. 1999b. *Morocco: Country Profile 1999–2000*. London: Economist Publications.

———. 2000a. *Algeria: Country Profile 2000*. London: Economist Publications.

———. 2000b. *Morocco: Country Profile 2000*. London: Economist Publications.

———. 2000c. *Syria: Country Profile 2000–2001*. London: Economist Publications.

———. 2000d. *Jordan: Country Profile 2000*. London: Economist Publications.

———. 2001a. *Jordan: Country Profile 2001*. London: Economist Publications.

———. 2001b. *Yemen: Country Profile 2001*. London: Economist Publications.

———. 2001c. *Tunisia: Country Profile 2001*. London: Economist Publications.

———. 2002. *Qatar: Country Profile 2002*. London: Economist Publications.

———. 2003a. *Jordan: Country Profile 2003*. London: Economist Publications.

———. 2003b. *Syria: Country Profile 2003*. London: Economist Publications.

———. 2003c. *Oman: Country Profile 2003*. London: Economist Publications.

———. 2003d. *Lebanon: Country Profile 2003*. London: Economist Publications.

———. 2004a. *Iraq: Country Report. June 2004*. London: Economist Publications.

———. 2004b. *Tunisia: Country Profile 2004*. London: Economist Publications.

———. 2004c. *Syria: Country Profile 2004*. London: Economist Publications.

———. 2005a. *Israel: Country Profile 2005*. London: Economist Publications.

———. 2005b. *Jordan: Country Profile 2005*. London: Economist Publications.

———. 2005c. *Kuwait: Country Profile 2005*. London: Economist Publications.

———. 2005d. *Morocco: Country Profile 2005*. London: Economist Publications.

———. 2005e. *Oman: Country Profile 2005*. London: Economist Publications.

———. 2005f. *Tunisia: Country Profile 2005*. London: Economist Publications.

———. 2005g. *UAE: Country Profile 2005*. London: Economist Publications.

———. 2005h. *Algeria: Country Profile 2005*. London: Economist Publications.

———. 2005i. *Syria: Country Profile 2005*. London: Economist Publications.

———. 2005j. *Yemen: Country Profile 2005*. London: Economist Publications.

———. 2005k. *Iraq: Country Profile 2005*. London: Economist Publications.

———. 2005l. *Qatar: Country Profile 2005*. London: Economist Publications.

———. 2005m. *Lebanon: Country Profile 2005*. London: Economist Publications.

———. 2006a. *Morocco: Country Profile 2006*. London: Economist Publications.

———. 2006b. *Syria: Country Profile 2006*. London: Economist Publications.

———. 2007a. *Algeria: Country Profile 2007*. London: Economist Publications.

———. 2007b. *Egypt: Country Profile 2007*. London: Economist Publications.

———. 2007c. *Iraq: Country Profile 2007*. London: Economist Publications.

———. 2007d. *Jordan: Country Profile 2007*. London: Economist Publications.

———. 2007e. *Morocco: Country Profile 2007*. London: Economist Publications.

———. 2007f. *Syria: Country Profile 2007*. London: Economist Publications.

———. 2007g. *Yemen: Country Profile 2007*. London: Economist Publications.

———. 2008a. *Algeria: Country Profile 2008*. London: Economist Publications.

———. 2008b. *Bahrain: Country Profile 2008*. London: Economist Publications.

———. 2008c. *Egypt: Country Profile 2008*. London: Economist Publications.

———. 2008d. *Iraq: Country Profile 2008*. London: Economist Publications.

———. 2008e. *Jordan: Country Profile 2008*. London: Economist Publications.

———. 2008f. *Morocco: Country Profile 2008*. London: Economist Publications.

———. 2008g. *Syria: Country Profile 2008*. London: Economist Publications.

———. 2008h. *Yemen: Country Profile 2008*. London: Economist Publications.

———. 2009. *Bahrain: Country Profile 2009*. London: Economist Publications.

Human Rights Watch. 2003. *Iraq: Forcible Expulsion of Ethnic Minorities 15(3) (E)*. New York: HRW.

———. 2004. *Claims in Conflict: Reversing Ethnic Conflict in Northern Iraq 16(4) (E)*. New York: HRW.

———. 2006. "UAE: Address Abuse of Migrant Workers." *Press release*, 20 March 2006.

IISS. "Various years." *The Military Balance*. London: International Institute for Strategic Studies.

IMF. 2004a. *Tunisia: Preliminary Findings of the Article IV Consultation Mission*. Washington, DC: International Monetary Fund.

———. 2004b. *United Arab Emirates: Article IV Consultations (Statistical Appendix SM/04/166*. Washington, DC: International Monetary Fund.

Kuwait. "Various years." *Annual Report*. Kuwait: Central Bank of Kuwait.

Lebanon. 1994. *Al-Taqrir al-sanawi li-aʿwam 1993/94 (Annual Report 1993/94)*. Beirut: Masrif Lubnan (Bank of Lebanon).

———. 2010. *Data and Statistics*. Beirut: Ministry of Finance. http://www .finance.gov.lb

Oman. 2000. *Al-Hasab Al-Khatami lil-daula (The State's Final Account of the Fiscal Year)*. Muscat: Ministry of Finance.

———. 2001. *Al-Hasab Al-Khatami lil-daula (The State's Final Account of the Fiscal Year)*. Muscat: Ministry of Finance.

———. 2002. *Al-Hasab Al-Khatami lil-daula (The State's Final Account of the Fiscal Year)*. Muscat: Ministry of Finance.

———. 2003. *Al-Hasab Al-Khatami lil-daula (The State's Final Account of the Fiscal Year)*. Muscat: Ministry of Finance.

———. 2005. *Annual Report*. Muscat: Central Bank of Oman.

———. 2007. *Annual Report*. Muscat: Central Bank of Oman.

———. 2008. *Annual Report*. Muscat: Central Bank of Oman.

Qatar. 2005. *Quarterly Statistical Bulletin*, September 2005. Doha: Central Bank of Qatar.

Saudi Arabia. 1998. *Thirty-Fourth Annual Report*. Riyadh: Saudi Arabian Monetary Agency.

———. 2005. *Forty-First Annual Report*. Riyadh: Saudi Arabian Monetary Agency.

Tunisia. 1999. *Rapport Annuel 1998*. Tunis: Central Bank of Tunisia.

UAE. 1999. *Abu Dhabi Fund for Development, Law No. 10 of 1999; Concerning the Establishment of Abu Dhabi Fund for Development*. Abu Dhabi: ADFD.

UAE Central Bank. "Various years." *Economic Bulletin*. Abu Dhabi: UAE Central Bank.

———. "Various years." *Statistical Bulletin*. Abu Dhabi: UAE Central Bank.

———. "Various years." *Annual Report*. Abu Dhabi: UAE Central Bank.

United Nations. 1995. *Statistical Yearbook (40th edition)*. New York: United Nations Publications.

———. 2005. *Report of the Special Rapporteur on the right to food, Jean Ziegler*. Geneva: Commission on Human Rights, Sixty-first session, E/CN.4/2005/47.

United Nations and Boutros Boutros-Ghali. 1992. *An Agenda for Peace. Preventive diplomacy, peacemaking and peace-keeping. Report of the Secretary-General pursuant to the statement adopted by the Summit Meeting of the Security Council on 31 January 1992*. New York, A/47/277—S/24111.

United Nations and Lakhdar Brahimi. 2000. *Report of the Panel on United Nations Peace Operations*. New York, A/55/305—S/2000/809.

United Nations Development Programme. 2004. *Arab Human Development Report 2003: Building A Knowledge Society*. New York: United Nations Publications.

———. 2005. *Arab Human Development Report 2004: Towards Freedom in the Arab World*. New York: United Nations Publications.

United States. 2005. *Measuring Stability and Security in Iraq. Report to Congress by Department of Defense*. Washington, DC: Department of Defense.

World Bank. 2003a. *Trade, Investment and Development in the Middle East and North Africa: Engaging with the World*. Washington, DC: World Bank.

———. 2003b. *Better Governance for Development in the Middle East and North Africa: Enhancing Inclusiveness and Accountability*. Washington, DC: World Bank.

Yemen. 2003. *Kitab al-Ihsa'i al-sanawiyya (Statistical yearbook)*. Sana': Central Statistical Organization.

———. 2004. *Kitab al-Ihsa'i al-sanawiyya (Statistical yearbook)*. Sana': Central Statistical Organization.

Articles and Books

Ahmad, Eqbal. 1982. "Comments on Skocpol." *Theory and Society* 11 (3): 293–300.

Al-Adhami, M. M. 1979. "The election for the constituent assembly in Iraq, 1922–24." In *The Integration of Modern Iraq*, ed. Abbas Kelidar, 13–31. London: Croom Helm.

Al-'Al, Ukashah 'Abd. 1996. "Markaz al-mar'a fi tashri' al-jinsiyya fi dawlat al- 'imarat al- 'arabiyya al-muttahida (Studies in the legal framework of natu-ralisation in the United Arab Emirates)." *Dirasat fi Mujtama' al-'imarat* 12: 173–202.

Al-Din, Ahmad Najm. 1970. *Ahwal al-Sukkan fi al-'Iraq (Conditions of the Popu-lation in Iraq)*. Cairo: Ma'had al-Buhuth wa-al-Dirasat al-'Arabiyah.

Al-Khafaji, Isam. 2000. "War as a vehicle for the rise and demise of a state-controlled society: The case of Ba'thist Iraq." In *War, Institutions, and Social Change in the Middle East*, ed. Steven Heydemann, 258–91. Berkeley, CA: University of California Press.

Al-Khalil, Samir. 1989. *Republic of Fear: Saddam's Iraq*. London: Hutchinson Ra-dius.

Al-Naqeeb, Khaldoun H. 1990. *Society and the State in the Gulf and the Arab Peninsula. A different perspective*. London: Routledge.

Alnasrawi, Abbas. 2001. "Iraq: Economic sanctions and consequences, 1990–2000." *Third World Quarterly* 22 (2): 205–19.

Al-Rukn, Muhammad. 2000. "Nahw 'i'adah nazar fi qanun al-jinsiyya (the method of appellate review in nationality law)" *Al-Khalij*, 24 January.

Al-Sabbagh, Salah al-Din. 1956. *Fursan al-'Urubah fi al-'Iraq (The Knights of Pan-Arabism in Iraq)*. Damascus: Al-Shabab al-'Arabi.

Al-Sayegh, Fatma. 1998. "Merchants' role in a changing society: The case of Dubai, 1900–90." *Middle Eastern Studies* 34 (1): 87–102.

Amawi, Abla M. 1993. *State and class in Transjordan: A study of state autonomy*. PhD thesis, Georgetown University.

Anderson, Betty. 2002. "The duality of national identity in the Middle East: A critical review." *Critique: Critical Middle Eastern Studies* 11 (2): 229–50.

———. 2003. "Review essay: The evolution of Jordanian studies." *Critique: Criti-cal Middle Eastern Studies* 12 (2): 197–202.

Askari, Hossein, John Cummings, and Michael Glover. 1982. *Taxation and Tax Policies in the Middle East*. London: Butterworth Scientific.

Axelrod, Lawrence. 1978. "Tribesmen in uniform: The demise of the Fidaiyyun in Jordan, 1970–71." *The Muslim World* 68 (1): 25–45.

Ayoob, Mohammed. 1996. *The Third World Security Predicament: State Making, Regional Conflict and the International System*. Boulder, CO: Lynne Rienner.

Ayubi, Nazih M. 1995. *Overstating the Arab State: Politics and Society in the Mid-dle East*. London: I. B. Tauris.

Bank, André, and Oliver Schlumberger. 2004. "Jordan: Between regime survival and economic reform." In *Arab Elites: Negotiating the Politics of Change*, ed. Volker Perthes, 35–60. Boulder, CO: Lynne Rienner.

Barnett, Michael N. 1992. *Confronting the Costs of War: Military Power, State, and Society in Egypt and Israel*. Princeton, NJ: Princeton University Press.

Barro, Robert J. 1997. *Determinants of Economic Growth: A Cross-Country Empirical Study*. Cambridge, MA: MIT Press.

———. 2000. *The Rule of Law, Democracy, and Economic Performance*. Washington, DC: Heritage Foundation.

Batatu, Hanna. 1978. *The Old Social Classes and the Revolutionary Movements of Iraq: A Study of Iraq's Old Landed and Commercial Classes and of its Communists, Baathists, and Free Officers*. Princeton, NJ: Princeton University Press.

Baylouny, Anne Marie. 2008. "Militarizing welfare: Neo-liberalism and Jordanian policy." *Middle East Journal* 62 (2): 277–303.

Beaugé, Gilbert. 1986. "La 'kafala': Un système de gestion transitoire de la main-œuvre et du capital dans les pays du Golfe (the 'kafala': a control system for labor and capital in the Gulf states)." *Revue Européenne des migrations internationales* 2 (1): 109–22.

Beblawi, Hazem. 1990. "The rentier state in the Arab world." In *The Arab State*, ed. Giacomo Luciani, 85–98. London: Routledge.

Bellin, Eva. 2002. *Stalled Democracy. Capital, Labor, and the Paradox of State-Sponsored Development*. Ithaca, NY: Cornell University Press.

Bennoune, Mahfoud. 1988. *The Making of Contemporary Algeria, 1830–1987*. Cambridge: Cambridge University Press.

Bocco, Riccardo. 1989. "L'Etat producteur d'identités locales: Lois électorales et tribus bédouines en Jordanie, 1929–1989 (the state as producer of local identities: electoral laws and Bedouin tribes in Jordan, 1929–1989)." In *Le nomade, l'oasis et la ville* (the nomade, the oasis and the city), ed. Jean Bisson, 271–88. Tours: URBAMA.

Bocco, Riccardo, and Tariq Tell. 1994. "Pax Britannica in the steppe: British policy and the Transjordan Bedouin." In *Village, Steppe and State: The Social Origins of Modern Jordan*, eds. Eugene Rogan and Tariq Tell, 108–27. London: British Academic Press.

Boix, Carles. 2003. *Democracy and Redistribution*. Cambridge: Cambridge University Press.

Brand, Laurie A. 1992. "Economic and political liberalization in a rentier economy: The case of the Hashemite Kingdom of Jordan." In *Privatization and Liberalization in the Middle East*, eds. Ilya Harik and Denis J. Sullivan, 167–88. Bloomington, IN: Indiana University Press.

———. 2001. "In search of budget security: A reexamination of Jordanian foreign policy." In *Diplomacy in the Middle East: The International Relations of Regional and Outside Powers*, ed. L. Carl Brown, 139–58. London: I. B. Tauris.

Brown, L. Carl. 1984. *International Politics of the Middle East: Old Rules, Dangerous Game*. Princeton, NJ: Princeton University Press.

Brown, Michael E., Sean M. Lynn-Jones, and Steven E. Miller, eds. 1996. *Debating the Democratic Peace*. Cambridge, MA: MIT Press.

Brown, Nathan J. 2002. *Constitutions in a Nonconstitutional World: Arab Basic Laws and the Prospects for Accountable Government.* New York: State University of New York Press.

Brownlee, Jason. 2002. " . . . and yet they persist: Explaining survival and transitions in neopatrimonial regimes." *Studies in Comparative International Development* 37 (3): 35–63.

Brumberg, Daniel. 2002. "The trap of liberalized autocracy." *Journal of Democracy* 13 (4): 56–68.

Brynen, Rex. 2000. *A Very Political Economy: Peacebuilding and Foreign Aid in the West Bank and Gaza.* Washington, DC: United States Institute of Peace.

Buchta, Wilfred. 2004. "Sayyid Ali al-Husain al-Sistani." *Orient* 45 (3): 343–55.

Burke, Edmund. 1790. *Reflections on the Revolution in France and on the Proceedings in Certain Societies in London (3rd edition)* London: Printed for J. Dodsley.

Butzclaar-Mohr, Françoise. 1992. "Maghreb: Taxation of Investment Income." *Bulletin for International Documentation* 46 (4): 206–9.

Caplan, Richard. 2005. *International Governance of War-Torn Territories: Rule and Reconstruction.* Oxford: Oxford University Press.

Centeno, Miguel Angel. 2002. *Blood and Debt: War and the Nation-State in Latin America.* University Park, PA: Pennsylvania State University Press.

Chaudhry, Kiren Aziz. 1990. "Economic liberalization in oil-exporting countries: Iraq and Saudi Arabia." In *Privatization and Liberalization in the Middle East*, eds. Ilya Harik and Denis J. Sullivan, 145–66. Bloomington, IN: Indiana University Press.

———. 1997. *The Price of Wealth: Economies and Institutions in the Middle East.* Ithaca, NY: Cornell University Press.

Chesterman, Simon. 2004. *You the People: The United Nations, Transitional Administration, and State-Building.* Oxford: Oxford University Press.

Chhibber, Pradeep K. 1996. "State policy, rent seeking, and the electoral success of a religious party in Algeria." *Journal of Politics* 58 (1): 126–48.

Clapham, Christopher. 1998. "Degrees of statehood." *Review of International Studies* 24 (2): 143–57.

Cooley, Alexander A. 2001. "Booms and busts: Theorizing institutional formation and change in oil states." *Review of International Political Economy* 8 (1): 163–80

Cooper, Christopher, and Greg Jaffe. 2004. "Iraqi spending prompts critique from UN Board." *Wall Street Journal Europe*, September 17–19, A1.

Cordesman, Anthony H. 2004. *The Military Balance in the Middle East.* Westport, CT: Praeger.

Crocker, Ryan. 2010. "Dreams of Babylon." *The National Interest* 108, 18–23.

Crystal, Jill. 1990. *Oil and Politics in the Gulf: Rulers and Merchants in Kuwait and Qatar.* Cambridge: Cambridge University Press.

Cunningham, Robert B., and Yasin K. Sarayrah. 1993. *Wasta: The Hidden Force in Middle Eastern Society.* Westport, CT: Praeger.

———. 1994. "Taming wasta to achieve development." *Arab Studies Quarterly* 16 (3): 29–41.

Czempiel, Ernst-Otto. 1981. *Internationale Politik: Ein Konfliktmodell (International Politics: A Model of Conflict).* Paderborn: Schöningh.

Dar al-Khalij lil-sihafa wa al-thiba'a wa al-nashr. 2001. *Al-Taqrir al-Istratijiyya al-khalijiyya, 2000–2001 (The Gulf Strategic Report 2000–2001).* Sharjah: Dar Al Khaleej Printing and Publishing.

David, Steven R. 1991. "Explaining Third World alignment." *World Politics* 43 (2): 233–56.

Day, Arthur R. 1986. *East Bank–West Bank: Jordan and the prospects for peace.* New York: Council on Foreign Relations.

Dodge, Toby. 2003. *Inventing Iraq: The Failure of Nation-Building and a History Denied.* New York: Columbia University Press.

———. 2004. *Iraq transition: Civil war or civil society?* Hearing before Committee on Foreign Relations, United States Senate, 108th Cong., 2nd session, April 20.

Doner, Richard F., Bryan K. Ritchie, and Dan Slater. 2005. "Systemic vulnerability and the origins of developmental states: Northeast and Southeast Asia in comparative perspective." *International Organization* 59 (2): 327–61.

Downing, Brian M. 1992. *The Military Revolution and Political Change: Origins of Democracy and Autocracy in Early Modern Europe.* Princeton, NJ: Princeton University Press.

Dresch, Paul. 2004. "Debates on marriage and nationality in the United Arab Emirates." In *Monarchies and Nations: Globalisation and Identity in the Arab States of the Gulf*, eds. Paul Dresch and James Piscatori, 136–57. London: I. B. Tauris.

Durra, Mahmud. 1969. *Al-Harb al-'iraqiyya al-britaniyya (The British–Iraqi War of 1941).* Beirut: Dar al-Tali'a.

Dutta, Ashok. 2005. "Another day in paradise." *Middle East Economic Digest*, July 15.

El-Edroos, Brigadier S. A. 1980. *The Hashemite Arab Army 1908–1979: An Appreciation and Analysis of Military Operations.* Amman: Publishing Committee.

El-Haj, Ribhi Abu. 1961. "Capital formation in Iraq, 1922–1957." *Economic Development and Cultural Change* 9 (4): 604–17.

Eppel, Michael. 1998. "The elite, the Effendiyya, and the growth of nationalism and pan-Arabism in Hashemite Iraq, 1921–1958." *International Journal of Middle East Studies* 30 (2): 227–50.

Ertman, Thomas. 1997. *Birth of the Leviathan: Building States and Regimes in Mediaeval and Early Modern Europe*. Cambridge: Cambridge University Press.

Fasano, Ugo. 2003. *Monetary Union among Member Countries of the Gulf Cooperation Council (Occasional Paper 223)*. Washington, DC: International Monetary Fund.

Fauvelle-Aymar, Christine. 1999. "The political and tax capacity of government in developing countries." *Kyklos* 52 (3): 391–413.

Finlan, Alaistair. 2005. "Trapped in the Dead Ground: US Counter-insurgency Strategy in Iraq." *Small Wars and Insurgencies* 16 (1): 1–21.

Frisch, Hillel. 2002. "Fuzzy nationalism: The case of Jordan." *Nationalism and Ethnic Politics* 8 (4): 86–103.

Fukuyama, Francis. 2004. *State Building: Governance and World Order in the Twenty-First Century*. Ithaca, NY: Cornell University Press.

Gause, Gregory. 1994. *Oil Monarchies: Domestic and Security Challenges in the Arab Gulf States*. New York: Council on Foreign Relations.

———. 2002. "Iraq's decision to go to war, 1980 and 1990." *Middle East Journal* 56 (1): 47–71.

Goldstone, Jack A., Ted Robert Gurr, Barbara Harff, Marc A. Levy, Monty G. Marshall, Robert H. Bates, David L. Epstein, Colin H. Kahl, Pamela T. Surko, John C. Ulfelder Jr, and Alan N. Unger. 2000. *State Failure Task Force Report: Phase III Findings*. McLean, VA: Science Applications International Corporation.

Gongora, Thierry. 1997. "War making and state power in the contemporary Middle East." *International Journal of Middle East Studies* 29, 323–40.

Gordon, Michael R., and Bernard E. Trainor. 2006. *Cobra II: The Inside Story of the Invasion and Occupation of Iraq*. New York: Pantheon Books.

Glubb, John Bagot. 1948. *The Story of the Arab Legion*. London: Hodder and Stoughton.

———. 1983. *The Changing Scenes of Life: An Autobiography*. London: Quartet.

Hadhri, Mohieddine. 1978. "Essai sur l'histoire du parti communiste irakien: Luttes nationales et stratégie internationaliste (Essay on the history of the Iraqi communist party: national struggle and international strategy)." In *Mouvement ouvrier: Communisme et nationalismes dans le monde arabe (labor movement: communism and nationalism in the Arab world)*, ed. René Gallissot, 203–29. Paris: Editions ouvrières.

Hasan, Mohammad Salman. 1958. *Foreign trade in the economic development of modern Iraq, 1869–1939*. DPhil thesis, St Anthony's College, Oxford University.

Hashim, Ahmed S. 2006. *Insurgency and Counter-Insurgency in Iraq*. London: Hurst.

Hay, Sir Rupert. 1954. "The Persian Gulf states and their boundary problems." *Geographical Journal* 120 (4): 433–45.

Heard-Bey, Frauke. 1996. *From Trucial States to United Arab Emirates: A Society in Transition*. London: Longman.

———. 2005. "The United Arab Emirates: Statehood and Nation-Building in a Traditional Society." *Middle East Journal* 59 (3): 357–75.

Helman, Gerald B., and Steven R. Ratner. 1992–93. "Saving failed states." *Foreign Policy* 84, 3–21.

Hemphill, Paul P. J. 1979. "The formation of the Iraqi Army, 1921–33." In *The Integration of Modern Iraq*, ed. Abbas Kelidar, 88–110. London: Croom Helm.

Herb, Michael. 1999. *All in the Family: Absolutism, Revolution, and Democracy in the Middle Eastern Monarchies*. New York: State University of New York Press.

———. 2003. "Taxation and representation." *Studies in Comparative International Development* 38 (3): 3–31.

Herbst, Jeffrey. 2000. *States and Power in Africa: Comparative Lessons in Authority and Control*. Princeton, NJ: Princeton University Press.

Hertog, Steffen. 2008. "Two-level negotiations in a fragmented system: Saudi Arabia's WTO accession." *Review of International Political Economy* 15 (4): 650–79.

Heydemann, Steven. 2000a. "War, institutions, and social change in the Middle East." In *War, Institutions, and Social Change in the Middle East*, ed. Steven Heydemann, 1–30. Berkeley, CA: University of California Press.

———, ed. 2000b. *War, Institutions, and Social Change in the Middle East*. Berkeley, CA: University of California Press.

Hood, Christopher. 2003. "The tax state in the information age." In *The Nation-State in Question*, eds. T. V. Paul, G. John Ikenberry, and John A. Hall, 213–27. Princeton, NJ: Princeton University Press.

Hoskins, Eric. 1997. "The humanitarian impacts of economic sanctions and war in Iraq." In *Political Gain and Civilian Pain. Humanitarian Impacts of Economic Sanctions*, ed. Thomas G. Weiss, 91–148. Lanham, MD: Rowman and Littlefield.

Ibn Khaldun. 1967 [1377]. *The Muqaddimah: An Introduction to History*. London: Routledge.

Ibrahim, Abu Yaqsan. 1978. *Al-Jinsira fi dawlat al-'imarat al-'arabiyya al-muttahida wa dirasa muqarina bil-jinsiyya fi duwal al-khalij (Naturalisation in the United Arab Emirates and studies in decisions on naturalisation in the Gulf States)*. Abu Dhabi: Wizarat al-i'lam wal-thaqafa.

Jensen, Nathan M. 2003. "Democratic governance and multinational corporations: Political regimes and inflows of foreign direct investment." *International Organization* 57 (3): 587–616.

Joyce, Miriam. 2003. *Ruling Shaikhs and Her Majesty's Government, 1960–1969.* London: Frank Cass.

Jreisat, Jamil E. 1989. "Bureaucracy and development in Jordan." *Journal of Asian and African Studies* 24 (1–2): 94–105.

Jung, Dietrich. 1997. "Das Kriegsgeschehen im Nahen Osten: 43 Kriege und ein Friedensprozeß (War in the Near East: 43 wars and one peace process)." *Orient* 38 (2): 337–51.

Kaldor, Mary. 1999. *New and Old Wars: Organized Violence in a Global Era.* Cambridge: Polity Press.

Karl, Terry Lynn. 1997. *The Paradox of Plenty: Oil Boom and Petro States.* Berkeley, CA: University of California Press.

Kelly, John Barrett. 1956. "The Buraimi Oasis dispute." *International Affairs (Royal Institute of International Affairs)* 32 (3): 318–26.

———. 1964. *Eastern Arabian Frontiers.* London: Faber and Faber.

———. 1968. *Britain and the Persian Gulf, 1795–1880.* Oxford: Oxford University Press.

Kilani, Sa'eda, and Basem Sakijha. 2000. *Towards Transparency in Jordan.* Amman: Arab Archives Institute.

———. 2002. *Wasta: The Declared Secret. A Study on Nepotism and Favouritism in Jordan.* Amman: Arab Archives Institute.

Kingston, Paul W. T. 1996. *Britain and the politics of modernization in the Middle East, 1945–1958.* Cambridge: Cambridge University Press.

Knowles, Warwick. 2005. *Jordan Since 1989: A Study in Political Economy.* London: I. B. Tauris.

Kosack, Stephen. 2003. "Effective aid: How democracy allows development aid to improve quality of life." *World Development* 31 (1): 1–22.

Krause, Keith. 1996. "Insecurity and state formation in the global military order: The Middle Eastern case." *European Journal of International Relations* 2 (3): 319–54.

Kuran, T. 1998. "The vulnerability of the Arab state: Reflections on the Ayubi thesis." *The Independent Review* 3 (1): 111–23.

Layne, Linda L. 1994. *Home and Homeland: The Dialogics of Tribal and Nationalism Identities in Jordan.* Princeton, NJ: Princeton University Press.

Leander, Anna. 2001. "Dependency today: Finance, firms, mafias and the state. A review of Susan Strange's work from a developing country perspective." *Third World Quarterly* 22 (1): 115–28.

———. 2004. "Wars and the unmaking of states: Taking Tilly seriously in the contemporary world." In *Copenhagen Peace Research: Conceptual Innovations and Contemporary Security Analysis,* eds. Stefano Guzzini and Dietrich Jung, 69–80. London: Routledge.

Levi, Margaret. 1988. *Of Rule and Revenue*. Berkeley, CA: University of California Press.

Linz, Juan J. 1975. "Totalitarian and authoritarian regimes." In *Handbook of Political Science, Vol. 3*, eds. Nelson Polsby and Fred Greenstein, 175–411. Reading, PA: Addison Wesley.

Linz, Juan J., Larry Diamond, and Seymour Lipset. 1988. *Democracy in Developing Countries. Vol. 2: Africa*. Boulder, CO: Westview.

Lipset, Seymour Martin. 1959. "Social requisites of democracy: Economic development and political legitimacy." *American Political Science Review* 53 (1): 69–105.

Lowi, Miriam R. 2004. "Oil rents and political breakdown in patrimonial states: Algeria in comparative perspective." *Journal of North African Studies* 9 (3): 83–102.

Luciani, Giacomo. 1990. "Allocation vs. production states: A theoretical framework." In *The Arab State*, ed. Giacomo Luciani, 65–84. London: Routledge.

———. 1994. "The oil rent, the fiscal crisis of the state and democratization." In *The Foundations of the Arab State*, ed. Ghassan Salamé, 130–55. London: Croom Helm.

Luizard, Pierre-Jean. 1994. "Les Irakiens à la recherche d'un nouveau contrat de coexistence (Iraqis in search of a new contract of coexistence)." In *Moyen-Orient: Migrations, Démocratisation, Médiations (Middle East: Migration, Democratization, Mediation)*, eds. Riccardo Bocco and Mohammad-Reza Djalili, 267–99. Paris: Presses Universitaire de France.

Lustick, Ian. 1997. "The absence of Middle Eastern Great Powers: Political 'backwardness' in historical perspective." *International Organization* 51 (4): 653–83.

Lynch, Marc. 2002. "Jordan's identity and interests." In *Identity and Foreign Policy in the Middle East*, eds. Shibley Telhami and Michael Barnett, 26–57. Ithaca, NY: Cornell University Press.

Mahdavy, Hossein. 1970. "The patterns and problems of economic development in rentier states: The case of Iran." In *Studies in the Economic History of the Middle East*, M. A. Cook, 428–67. London: Oxford University Press.

Mann, Michael. 1993. *The Sources of Social Power, Vol. 2*. Cambridge: Cambridge University Press.

Mansur, Ahsan, and Volker Treichel. 1999. *Oman Beyond the Oil Horizon: Policies Toward Sustainable Growth (Occasional Paper 185)*. Washington, DC: International Monetary Fund.

Massad, Joseph A. 2001. *Colonial Effects: The Making of National Identity in Jordan*. New York: Columbia University Press.

McNeill, William. 1983. *The Pursuit of Power: Technology, Armed Force, and Society since AD 1000*. Oxford: Oxford University Press.

Metz, Steven. 2010. *Decisionmaking in Operation Iraqi Freedom: The Strategic Shift of 2007*. Carlisle, PA: United States Army War College, Strategic Studies Institute.

Migdal, Joel. 1988. *Strong Societies and Weak States: State–Society Relations and State Capabilities in the Third World*. Princeton, NJ: Princeton University Press.

———. 2001. *State in Society: Studying How States and Societies Transform and Constitute One Another*. Cambridge: Cambridge University Press.

———. 2004. "State-building and the non-nation-state." *Journal of International Affairs* 58 (1), 7–46.

Milliken, Jennifer, and Keith Krause. 2002. "State failure, state collapse, and state reconstruction: Concepts, lessons and strategies." *Development and Change* 33 (5): 753–74.

Milton-Edwards, Beverly, and Peter Hinchcliffe. 1999. "Abdallah's Jordan: New king, old problems." *Middle East Report* 213, 28–31.

Mishal, Shaul. 1980. "Conflictual pressures and cooperative interests: Observations on West Bank–Amman political relations, 1949–1967." In *Palestinian Society and Politics*, ed. Joel S. Migdal, 69–82. Princeton, NJ: Princeton University Press.

Mobley, Richard A. 2004. "The Tunbs and Abu Musa Islands: Britain's perspective." *Middle East Journal* 57 (4): 627–45.

Mofid, Kamran. 1990. *The Economic Consequences of the Gulf War*. London: Routledge.

Moore, Mick. 2004. "Revenues, state formation, and the quality of governance in developing countries." *International Political Science Review* 25 (3): 297–319.

Moore, Pete W. 2003. "The newest Jordan: Free trade, peace and an ace in the hole." *Middle East Report online* June 26. http://www.merip.org/mero/mero062603.html.

———. 2004. *Doing Business in the Middle East: Politics and Economic Crisis in Jordan and Kuwait*. Cambridge: Cambridge University Press.

Noreng, Øystein. 2004. "The predicament of the Gulf rentier states." In *Oil in the Gulf: Obstacles to Democracy and Development*, eds. Daniel Heradstveit and Helge Hveem, 9–40. Aldershot: Ashgate.

North, Douglas, John Joseph Wallis, and Barry R. Weingast. 2009. *Violence and Social Orders: A Conceptual Framework for Interpreting Recorded Human History*. New York: Cambridge University Press.

Owen, Roger. 2000. "The cumulative impact of Middle Eastern wars." In *War, Institutions, and Social Change in the Middle East*, ed. Steven Heydemann, 325–34. Berkeley, CA: University of California Press.

Peake, F. G. 1958. *A History of Jordan and its Tribes*. Coral Gables, FL: University of Miami Press.

Perthes, Volker. 1995. *The Political Economy of Syria under Assad*. London: I. B. Tauris.

Pollack, Kenneth M. 2002. *Arabs at War: Military Effectiveness, 1948–1991*. Lincoln, NE: University of Nebraska Press.

Posch, Walter. 2005. *Looking into Iraq*. Paris: European Union Institute for Security Studies.

Pouligny, Béatrice. 2005. "Civil society and post-conflict peacebuilding: Ambiguities of international programmes aimed at building 'new' societies." *Security Dialogue* 36 (4): 495–510.

Przeworski, Adam, Michael E. Alvarez, José Antonio Cheibub, and Fernando Limongi. 2000. *Democracy and Development: Political Institutions and Well Being in the World, 1950–1990*. Cambridge: Cambridge University Press.

Putnam, Robert D. 1993. *Making Democracy Work: Civic Traditions in Modern Italy*. Princeton, NJ: Princeton University Press.

Qubain, Fahim. 1958. *The Reconstruction of Iraq, 1950–1957*. London: Atlantic Books.

Rasler, Karen A., and William R. Thompson. 1985. "War making and state making: Governmental expenditures, tax revenues, and global wars." *American Political Science Review* 79 (2),: 491–507.

Razoux, Pierre. 1999. *La Guerre Israélo-Arabe d'Octobre 1973 (The Israeli-Arab War of October 1973)*. Paris: Economica.

Richards, Alan, and John Waterbury. 1996. *A Political Economy of the Middle East*. Boulder, CO: Westview.

Richter, Thomas. 2004. *Determinanten einer Wirtschaftspolitik für Kleinst-, Klein- und Mittelunternehmen (KKMU) in Ägypten (Conditions of economic policy for small and medium enterprises in Egypt)*. Münster: LIT Verlag.

Ricks, Thomas E. 2006. *Fiasco: The American Military Adventure in Iraq*. New York: Penguin Press.

Rizvi, S. N. Asad. 1993. "From tents to high rise: Economic development of the United Arab Emirates." *Middle Eastern Studies* 29 (4): 664–78.

Robins, Philip. 2004. *A History of Jordan*. Cambridge: Cambridge University Press.

Ross, Michael L. 2001. "Does oil hinder democracy?" *World Politics* 53 (3): 325–61.

Rotberg, Robert I. ed. 2004. *When States Fail: Causes and Consequences*. Princeton, NJ: Princeton University Press.

Sadowski, Yahya. 1993. *Scuds or Butter? The Political Economy of Arms Control in the Middle East*. Washington, DC: Brookings Institution.

Salamé, Ghassan. 1987. "'Strong' and 'weak' states: A qualified return to the Muqaddimah." In *The Foundations of the Arab State*, ed. Ghassan Salamé, 205–40. London: Croom Helm).

———, ed. 1994. *Democracy Without Democrats? The Renewal of Politics in the Muslim World*. London: I. B. Tauris.

Satloff, Robert B. 1994. *From Abdullah to Hussein: Jordan in Transition*. New York: Oxford University Press.

Schlumberger, Oliver. 2000. "Arab political economy and the European Union's Mediterranean policy: What prospects for development?" *New Political Economy* 5 (2): 247–68.

———, ed. 2007. *Debating Arab Authoritarianism: Dynamics and Durability in Non-Democratic Regimes*. Stanford, CA: Stanford University Press.

———. 2008. "Structural reform, economic order, and development: Patrimonial capitalism." *Review of International Political Economy* 15 (4): 622–49.

Schlumberger, Oliver, and André Bank. 2002. "Succession, legitimacy, and regime stability in Jordan." *Arab Studies Journal* 9 (2): 50–73.

Schofield, Richard, and Gerald Blake. eds. 1988. *Arabian Boundaries: Primary Documents, 1853–1957. Vol. 1: General Issues of Political Control and Sovereignty I*. London: Archive Editions.

Schwarz, Rolf. 2004. *The Israeli–Jordanian Water Regime: A Model for Resolving Water Conflicts in the Jordan River Basin? (Occasional Paper 1/2004)*. Geneva: Programme for Strategic and International Security Studies.

———. 2005. "Post-conflict peace-building: The challenges of security, welfare and representation." *Security Dialogue* 36 (4): 429–46.

———. 2008a. "The political economy of state-formation in the Arab Middle East: Rentier states, economic reform, and democratization." *Review of International Political Economy* 15 (4): 599–621.

———. 2008b. "Introduction: Resistance to globalization in the Arab Middle East." *Review of International Political Economy* 15 (4): 590–98.

———. 2010. "NATO and Prevention of State Failure." *Contemporary Security Policy* 31 (2): 339–62.

Schwedler, Jillian. 2002. "Don't blink: Jordan's democratic opening and closing." *Middle East Report online*, July 3. http://www.merip.org/mero/mero070302.html

Sexton, Finbarr. 1994. "Taxation regime for foreign entities following the fundamental reform of existing income tax regulations." *Bulletin for International Fiscal Documentation* 49 (1): 14–20.

Sharabi, Hisham. 1988. *Neopatriarchy: A Theory of Distorted Change in Arab Society*. Oxford: Oxford University Press.

Sharif, Siham Kamil. 1968. "Income tax in Iraq." *Bulletin of International Fiscal Documentation* 22 (12): 543–55.

Shyrock, Andrew. 2000. "Popular genealogical nationalism: History writing and identity among the Balqa tribes of Jordan." *Comparative Studies in Society and History* 37 (2): 325–57.

Skinner, Quentin. 1989. "The State." In *Political Innovation and Conceptual Change*, eds. Terence Ball, James Farr, and Russell L. Hanson, 90–131. Cambridge: Cambridge University Press.

Skocpol, Theda. 1982. "Rentier state and Shi'a Islam in the Iranian Revolution." *Theory and Society* 11 (3): 265–83.

Sluglett, Peter. 1976. *Britain in Iraq, 1914–1932*. London: Ithaca Press.

Sluglett, Peter, and Marion Farouk-Sluglett. 1978. "Some reflections on the Sunni/Shi'i question in Iraq." *British Society for Middle Eastern Studies Bulletin* 5 (2): 79–87.

———. 1990. "Iraq since 1986: The strengthening of Saddam." *Middle East Report* 167, 19–24.

Smith, Benjamin. 2004. "Oil wealth and regime survival in the developing world, 1960–1999." *American Journal of Political Science* 48 (2): 232–46.

———. 2007. *Hard Times in the Land of Plenty: Oil Politics in Iran and Indonesia*. Ithaca, NY: Cornell University Press.

Snyder, Jack. 2010. "The state and violence: A discussion of violence and social orders. A conceptual framework for interpreting recorded human history." *Perspectives on Politics* 8 (1): 287–9.

Sørensen, Georg. 2001. "War and state making: Why doesn't it work in the Third World?" *Security Dialogue* 32 (3): 341–54.

Springborg, Robert, and Clement M. Henry. 2001. *Globalization and the Politics of Development in the Middle East*. Cambridge: Cambridge University Press.

Strang, David. 1991. "Anomaly and commonplace in European political expansion: Realist and institutional accounts." *International Organization* 45 (1): 143–62.

Strange, Susan. 1996. *The Retreat of the State: The Diffusion of Power in the World Economy*. Cambridge: Cambridge University Press.

Strayer, Joseph R. 1970. *On the Medieval Origins of the Modern State*. Princeton, NJ: Princeton University Press.

Susser, Asher. 2000. *Jordan: Case Study of a Pivotal State*. Washington, DC: Washington Institute of Near East Policy.

Taylor, Brian, and Roxana Botea. 2008. "Tilly tally: War-making and state-making in the contemporary Third World." *International Studies Review* 10 (1): 27–56.

Tell, Tariq. 2000. *The Social Origins of Hashemite Rule: Bedouin, Fallah and State on the East Bank*. DPhil thesis, Trinity College, Oxford University

Tilly, Charles, ed. 1975. *The Formation of National States in Western Europe*. Princeton, NJ: Princeton University Press.

———. 1985. "War making and state making as organized crime." In *Bringing the State Back In*, eds. Evans, Peter B.; Dietrich Rueschemeyer, and Theda Skocpol, 169–91. Cambridge: Cambridge University Press.

———. 1990. *Coercion, Capital and European States, AD 990–1990*. Oxford: Blackwell.

———. 2007a. "Extraction and democracy." In *The New Fiscal Sociology: Taxation in Comparative and Historical Perspective*, eds. Isaac William Martin, Ajay K. Mehrotra, and Monica Prasad, 173–82. New York: Cambridge University Press.

———. 2007b. "Etats forts, faibles, et birnbaumiens (Strong, weak and birnbaumian states)." In *Le temps de l'état: mélanges en l'honneur de Pierre Birnbaum (The time of the state: contributions in honor of Pierre Birnbaum)*, ed. Yves Déloye, 303–10. Paris: Fayard).

———. 2009. "Grudging consent." Originally published in *The American Interest* (October 2007): 17–23. http://essays.ssrc.org/tilly/wp-content/uploads/2009/05/tilly-grudging-consent.pdf.

Van Bruinessen, Martin. 2005. "Kurdish challenges." In *Looking into Iraq*, ed. Walter Posch, 45–72. Paris: European Union Institute for Security Studies.

Van Creveld, Martin. 1991. *The Transformation of War*. New York: Free Press.

———. 1999. *The Rise and Decline of the State*. Cambridge: Cambridge University Press.

Vandewalle, Dirk. 1998. *Libya since Independence: Oil and State Building*. Ithaca, NY: Cornell University Press.

Vatikiotis, P. J. 1967. *Politics and the Military in Jordan: A Study of the Arab Legion, 1921–1957*. London: Frank Cass.

Walker, Julian F. 1994. *The UAE: Internal Boundaries and the Boundary with Oman (Studies in Arabian Geopolitics 4)*. London: Archive Editions.

Waterbury, John. 1997. "From social contracts to extraction contracts: The political economy of authoritarianism and democracy." In *Islam, Democracy, and the State in North Africa*, ed. John Entelis, 141–76. Bloomington, IN: Indiana University Press.

———. 1998. "The state and economic transition in the Middle East and North Africa." In *Prospects for Middle Eastern and North African Economies: From Boom to Bust and Back?*, ed. Nemat Shafik, 159–77. Houndmills: Macmillan.

Weber, Max. 1922. *Grundriss der Sozialökonomie. Vol. 3: Wirtschaft und Gesellschaft (Foundations of Social Economy. Vol. 3: Economy and Society)*. Tübingen: Mohr Siebeck.

West, Bing. 2009. *The Strongest Tribe. War, Politics, and the Endgame in Iraq*. New York: Random House.

Wicksell, Knut. 1988. "A new principle of just taxation." In *Public Choice and Constitutional Economics*, eds. James Gwartney and Richard Wagner, 117–30. London: Jai Press.

Wilson, Heather. 1988. *International Law and the Use of Force by National Liberation Movements*. Oxford: Clarendon Press.

Wolf, Martin. 2004. *Why Globalization Works*. New Haven, CT: Yale University Press.

Yapp, Malcom E. 1991. *The Near East since the First World War*. London: Longman.

Zartman, William I. ed. 1995. *Collapsed States: The Disintegration and Restoration of Legitimate Authority*. Boulder, CO: Lynne Rienner.

Index

Rolf Schwarz is professor at the NATO Defense College in Rome.

Governance and International Relations in the Middle East
Edited by Mohsen M. Milani, University of South Florida

The University Press of Florida proudly announces a new, multidisciplinary series that explores the processes, structures, outcomes, and consequences of governance in the age of globalization in the Middle East. Governance is increasingly recognized as a critical element that simultaneously influences and is influenced by political, economic, social, religious, cultural, and global factors. Such factors include, but are not limited to, the nature and structural configuration of the state, leadership quality of the governing elites, role of non-governmental institutions and religion, the mass media, corruption, democratization, and foreign relations of the nation states.

Inter-Arab Alliances: Regime Security and Jordanian Foreign Policy, by Curtis R. Ryan (2009)

Contentious Politics in the Middle East: Political Opposition under Authoritarianism, edited by Holger Albrecht (2010)

War and State Building in the Middle East, by Rolf Schwarz (2012; first paperback edition, 2013)

www.ingramcontent.com/pod-product-compliance
Lightning Source LLC
Chambersburg PA
CBHW032352280326
41935CB00008B/549